The Ways of Prayer:

An Introduction

The Ways of Prayer:
An Introduction

Michael Francis
PENNOCK

AVE MARIA PRESS Notre Dame, IN 46556

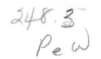

Library of Congress Catalog Card Number: 87-70971

Printed and bound in the United States of America.

Library of Congress Cataloging-in-Publication Data

Pennock, Michael.
    The ways of prayer.

    Bibliography: p.
    1. Prayer. 2. Spiritual life—Catholic authors.
I. Title.
BV215.P46   1987   248.3′2   87-1499
ISBN 0-87793-358-8 (pbk.)

Dedication

With love and gratitude to the Mooney family—

- René and Larry, an extraordinary Christian couple who inspire everyone who has ever been privileged to meet them and

- their outstanding children, Pete, Paul, John, Matt ("Moondog"), all former students of mine, Amy and Mark and

- their son Jimmy who, in a special way, has graced my ministry with his friendship and responsiveness to the Lord.

May the Lord continue to bless them all.

Acknowledgments

In a very special way, I wish to thank Joan Marie Bellina, my editor at Ave Maria Press. I am one of those very lucky authors who has been fortunate to link up with an intelligent, sensitive and visionary editor whose behind-the-scenes labors will never be properly recognized except by the Lord. I am indebted to Joan for her invaluable assistance on this book and her outstanding work on many of my other projects. May the Lord truly bless her for the inspiration and support she provides to those of us who are working in his vineyard.

I also wish to thank my loving wife, Carol, and our four children, Scott Michael, Jennifer Carol, Amy Marie and Christopher Joseph. Their love sustains and nourishes me.

Finally, I wish to thank our Lord for sending so many signs of his love into my life—my parents, my brothers and sisters and relatives, my friends and colleagues, my teachers and students. These many good people have taught me much about prayer and about the need to proclaim thanks and praise to our loving Father for his goodness.

Contents

Introduction

Prayer, like life, is a unique journey. No one else has walked my exact path. The special people in my life are different from those persons who are precious to another. The significant events in my life will inevitably be different from the key happenings in another person's life.

Prayer too is very personal. In fact, a common definition of prayer is *the deepening of one's personal relationship with God.* How the Lord meets and speaks with each of us is deeply personal; God relates to each of us in a special way.

In a certain sense, we too are prayers. We are in relationship to God merely because he has made us and keeps us in existence. Each of us is a word of God, speaking God's love and goodness to the rest of the world. Each of us prays—relates to God—in special and deeply personal ways; each of us is a unique prayer God has given to the human family.

This idea of being a prayer is new to most of us. We often think of prayer as a conversation with God. Prayer, of course, involves talking with and listening to the Lord. But prayer, like life, is much more; we can never exhaust its meaning. By praying, we continuously discover what God has already given us. Prayer deepens what we already have—a life with God—and helps us appreciate it even more.

Many of us have difficulty praying. We find the important things of the world claiming so much of our attention and time that we are diverted from the essential things in life. "It is only with the heart that one can see rightly;

what is essential is invisible to the eye."[1] What is essential to praying, and living life to the full, is also invisible to the eye; it is a matter of loving.

To materially oriented minds, this statement at first appears absurd. Yet as I strike the keys on my word processor, words mysteriously appear on the screen. They appear because of the complex internal workings of my computer, a process I don't understand. I can't see what's going on behind the scenes, so to speak, but I know that what I can't see is essential to words appearing on the screen.

"What is essential is invisible to the eye." The years of hard work in school merit the lawyer the knowledge and skill to defend her client. The powerful memory of a deceased parent often takes the adult son or daughter to the cemetery to pay regards.

That which is unseen provides powerful motivation. A mother goes through the same routine on behalf of her family for what appears to be the ten-thousandth time. What could possibly motivate her behavior? The material, visible rewards certainly aren't at all evident. Love is the essential ingredient which empowers her to be faithful to her family.

Some people say that seeing is believing. The reverse is true where love and prayer are involved: Believing is seeing. Love is essential for a full human life. Love is a spiritual reality which can't be measured using ordinary human instruments of perception. It can be sensed only with the heart.

Prayer is like love. It is a matter of the heart, a heart which longs for greater union with God. God loves me— that is the most essential truth of all. Realizing this truth and reminding ourselves of it can motivate us to pray. And even wanting to pray, to deepen our life with God, is itself a prayer. Prayer helps us realize and enjoy ever more

---

[1] Antoine de Saint-Exupery, *The Little Prince,* trans. Katherine Woods (New York: Harcourt Brace & Jovanovich, 1982).

deeply the Lord and the wonderful life of friendship to which he calls us.

This book is a short introduction to prayer for busy people, people who have a basic desire to pray but perhaps need a little guidance on how to get started. It begins with a few short definitions to show that prayer is very much a part of life, as natural as conversation and as varied as our moods and desires. We don't have to lock ourselves up in a cloister to pray. Prayer is a part of everyday life.

The book then suggests some practical ways we can get started in prayer—how to find a good time and place to pray, how to relax, how to listen for the Lord speaking to us, how to deal with distractions.

The next chapter looks to Jesus as a trusty guide for our prayer. His own personal example and his direct teaching on prayer offer much practical wisdom about communicating with his Father.

The following two chapters discuss several traditional methods of praying including meditation and contemplation, the Rosary, and methods taught by popular saints like St. Benedict, St. Francis of Assisi and St. Therese of Lisieux. The book encourages the reader to experiment with these methods in the hope that one or more of them will be helpful in contacting the living Lord.

A chapter introducing some of the spiritual classics which have inspired many Christian sojourners through the centuries is followed by a discussion of how to pray with and for others, emphasizing especially the eucharistic celebration.

The concluding chapters of the book include some additional popular prayer practices, some traditional prayers, and a short bibliography.

A Prayer Reflection

Each chapter of this book concludes with a short prayer reflection or exercise. The following prayer reflection helps put us in touch with the inner reality of God's love.

1. Briefly call to mind how much God loves you. Put yourself in his presence.

2. Ask the Holy Spirit to help you hear the Lord speaking to you in the scripture passage you will read.

3. Read Matthew 6:25-34 slowly. Hear the Lord telling you not to worry. Picture the care he bestows on the birds in the sky and on the colorful flowers that brighten the fields. Reflect on what the Lord says about you.

4. When you finish your silent reflection, honestly consider the things that you tend to worry about—your job, your appearance, how others relate to you, your health, your future. Are these things really worth worrying about? Has worrying ever helped? Then reflect on how valuable you are to yourself, your family, your friends, and especially to your heavenly Father.

A Scripture Reflection

Do not be afraid, for I have redeemed you;
I have called you by your name, you are mine.
Should you pass through the waters, I shall be with you;
or through rivers, they will not swallow you up.
Should you walk through fire, you will not suffer,
and the flame will not burn you.
For I am Yahweh, your God,
the Holy One of Israel, your Savior (Is 43:1-3).

1

Conversation With God

One of the most famous definitions of prayer comes from St. Clement. He defined prayer as "conversation with God." This is particularly apt because *conversation* implies an ongoing and developing relationship. We can get caught up in conversation, our attention totally focussed.

The Lord wants us to talk to him. Like any good friend, he is available to share our thoughts and our feelings, our hopes and our fears, our life and our love. God is always present and open to us. God is, to borrow an image from St. Teresa of Avila, an ever-present companion walking next to us along the path of life.

There are times when we can express ourselves to God spontaneously, much as we would to a close friend. The words flow in an atmosphere of love and trust, and we pray simply in words that come from the heart. Other times we are drawn to express ourselves using formal prayers, the traditional words of our Christian community. In either case we come to our conversation with God with a loving openness and trust that our relationship with him will deepen.

True conversation, of course, requires listening as well as talking. We need silent moments of listening if we are to "hear" God speaking to us.

The Lord "speaks" to us in many ways; we need to be sure that the many distractions of our lives don't keep us from hearing what he is saying. God's words surround us. He speaks to us in all created things—sunsets and sunrises, gentle rains, cooling breezes. He addresses us in the events and the people who come to us in our everyday lives. And the Father speaks to us in a very special way through Jesus who lives in scripture, in the Eucharist, and in the people we meet. We need only listen, remaining silent and letting God reveal in the depths of our hearts exactly what he is saying to us.

Indeed, I have found the Lord vitally present in the people he sends into my life, often in my high school students. I do try to see the Lord speaking to me through these students, young people who are brothers and sisters to me. But I sometimes suffer from loss of memory. I forget what I am doing and why I am doing it. On days when the students don't seem responsive, or when I feel lonely teaching in a classroom isolated from other adults, I don't readily listen for the Lord's word. Yet it is precisely then that the Lord speaks to me in a special way through one of my students.

Most recently I was enabled to see and hear the Lord through Jimmy. His cheerful attitude, enthusiasm for learning about his faith, and warm personality all affirmed me. But it was in the journal he kept for a course I was teaching on the fundamentals of prayer that Jimmy also revealed himself to be a faithful, mature pray-er. Reading his journal and subsequently talking to him about his prayer life became a powerful word of the Lord to me. His fidelity in prayer and his obvious love of the Lord renewed my own commitment to teach and learn from my students; his commitment to grow in the spiritual life challenged me to be a more authentic and diligent pray-er myself. Jimmy has enlivened my ministry, reminded me of the value of what I teach, affirmed me as a person, and taught me to be ever more faithful as a teacher of the Lord's word.

Conversation led me to meet and know Jimmy on a deep level. This is also true of our conversation, our prayer, with God. We can meet God alone as we do when we talk with him "behind closed doors" or simply withdraw and enjoy his presence without words. Or we can meet God with others in the sacraments, in prayer services, in any communal celebration of our relationship with our God. Prayer can be seen, then, as a true encounter with the Lord.

And prayer takes us still further. We converse with the Lord, we truly encounter him, and we live with him. God is always with us, and prayer is a continuous reminder that we are in the presence of this friend who loves us very much. As St. Paul says:

> Always be joyful; pray constantly; and for all things give thanks; this is the will of God for you in Christ Jesus (1 Thes 5:16-18).

Kinds of Prayer

Traditionally we have spoken of four kinds of prayer: adoration, contrition, thanksgiving and supplication.

Our prayers of *adoration* express our wonder and praise for God's love, wisdom, greatness, the beauty of his creation. We share our joy in the bounty of our Creator. We may pray spontaneously or turn to the Psalms, the prayer book of the Jewish and Christian religions, for words of praise, for example,

> Alleluia!

> Praise Yahweh from the heavens,
> praise him in the heights.
> Praise him, all his angels,
> praise him, all his host!

> Praise him, sun and moon,
> praise him, all shining stars,

praise him, highest heavens,
praise him, waters above the heavens.

Let them praise the name of Yahweh (Ps 148:1-5).

Prayers of *contrition* are expressions of sorrow for sins we have committed. In realization of God's goodness, we are moved to confess our sinfulness and ask for God's forgiveness. We look into our hearts and see our failures to love God above all things. Perhaps we have followed the false gods of pleasure or money. Perhaps we have let selfishness get in the way of our relationships with family and friends. Perhaps we have been indifferent to the poor and suffering of the world, the "little ones" of God. Perhaps we have misused God's bountiful creation. We confess our sinfulness in our own hearts and our own words, or we may use a formal act of contrition such as this:

O God,
I am sorry with my whole heart for all my sins
because you are goodness itself
and sin is an offense against you.
Therefore, I firmly resolve,
with the help of your grace,
not to sin again and to avoid the occasions of sin.

Prayers of *thanksgiving* are expressions of gratitude to God for all he has done for us. They acknowledge the many gifts he has given us: all of creation, our family and friends, our health and talents, the Lord Jesus, our salvation, the gift of the Holy Spirit, everything.

When we pray in thanksgiving we show that we don't take things for granted. When we thank God, we tell him how much we appreciate everything he has done for us. Without God we are nothing; we would not even have existence. We can find many beautiful expressions of thanksgiving such as these from the psalms:

Give thanks to Yahweh for he is good,
his faithful love lasts for ever (Ps 107:1).

I thank you, Yahweh, with all my heart,
for you have listened to the cry I uttered.
In the presence of angels I sing to you,
I bow down before your holy Temple.

I praise your name for your faithful love and your
    constancy;
your promises surpass even your fame (Ps 138:1-2a).

The most common form of prayer is *supplication*. Most of us take to heart the Lord's teaching,

"If you ask me for anything in my name,
I will do it" (Jn 14:14).

We ask for all kinds of things: good health for ourselves and our friends and families, peace and justice in the world, strength and patience when things are going poorly for us, a sunny day for a picnic. We count on Jesus' message that his Father is also our loving Father whom we may approach in confidence:

Our fearlessness towards him consists in this,
that if we ask anything in accordance with his will
he hears us.
And if we know that he listens to whatever we ask
    him,
we know that we already possess whatever we have
    asked of him (1 Jn 5:14-15).

Benefits of Praying

We pray not only to adore and thank God, not only to ask him for things or to express sorrow, not just because Jesus asks us to. We also pray because we get something, something of great value, out of it.

Many of us are like the apostle Thomas who had to see the Lord's wounds before he would believe that Jesus was raised from the dead. We want to know more, feel more secure, before we commit ourselves to a life of prayer.

We do have the promise of the Lord himself that

prayer will deepen our relationship to God. In addition, pray-ers mention the following benefits of living a life of prayer:

- *Prayer contributes to a sense of self-worth.*   In prayer we get in touch with our real selves. We discover that God loves us and that he abides with us. As we experience God's love and acceptance, we come to know our own worth and importance.

- *Prayer leads to happiness.*   We live in an age when people actively pursue happiness. But all too often we look in the wrong place, in material possessions or money or sex or power. We inevitably find, as people throughout the ages have found, that these things can satisfy us only for a time. In prayer we discover that our true source of enduring happiness is God; only he can fulfill the secret longings of our heart. As St. Augustine said, "Our hearts are restless until they rest in Thee."

- *Prayer changes us.*   We cannot meet the living God and remain unaffected. As the Danish theologian Soren Kierkegaard observed, "Prayer does not change God, but changes the one who prays." Prayer produces virtues in the one who prays. These virtues include faith, hope, love, humility, sensitivity to others, a compassionate heart and a desire to work for God's kingdom.

- *Prayer gives us more energy.*   Busy people, and that includes most of us, are always "on the go." We often seem to need more than 24 hours in a day. But pray-ers have discovered that time spent with the Lord is energizing. After prayer we return to our tasks with renewed enthusiasm and spirit. Prayer has a calming effect and renews us for the many tasks of the day that have to be done. In addition, time with the

Lord helps us sort our priorities so that we do not get caught up with society's values rather than our own.

• *Prayer has a healing effect.*   When we meet the Divine Physician in prayer, we are healed. He touches and cures our emotional hurts. He forgives our sin and relieves our guilt over harm we have caused.

• *Prayer helps solve our problems.*   We spend time and energy in needless worry about our problems. Prayer often helps us find our center and gain the insights we need to constructively work through our difficulties. In prayer we learn to "Let go and let God."

The greatest benefit of prayer, however, is the deepening of our relationship with God who loves us very much. We will only deepen our relationship with our divine friend if we take the risk and have the courage to pray.

A Prayer Reflection

Compose your own prayer. Use the traditional format with these four parts:

1.   an opening address, calling God by name;

2.   praise;

3.   thanksgiving;

4.   a petition.

Think a while about each category.

How do you want to address God today? Father? Mother? Almighty God? Abba? Lord? King of Kings? Divine Healer? Friend?

For what do you want to praise God? Are you especially grateful today for the beauty of creation? for God's

power and majesty? for God's goodness? mercy? love?
care?

For what would you like to thank God today? Success
in your job? a loving family? loyal friends? a good education? strength to carry on in a difficult situation?

What current need would you like to speak of? Family
strife? lack of appreciation at work? poor health? world
problems?

Meditating on these categories can be your prayer, or
you may choose to write a prayer in your journal.

A Scripture Reflection

God, you are my God, I pine for you;
my heart thirsts for you,
my body longs for you,
as a land parched, dreary and waterless.
Thus I have gazed on you in the sanctuary,
seeing your power and your glory.

Better your faithful love than life itself;
my lips will praise you.
Thus I will bless you all my life,
in your name lift up my hands.
All my longings fulfilled as with fat and rich foods,
a song of joy on my lips and praise in my mouth
    (Ps 63:1-5).

2

Getting Started in Prayer

Good preparation helps in any human endeavor. So it is with prayer. Anyone can pray, and everyone should pray. Although prayer does not take tremendous discipline or a great deal of preparation, masters of the spiritual life suggest some preparation so that our meetings with the Lord will bear good fruit.

Beginning pray-ers should cultivate a good attitude toward prayer, find a regular time and place to pray, and learn how to relax to facilitate their meeting with the Lord.

The Right Attitude

Perhaps the most important element in preparing to pray is attitude. One of the traditional definitions of prayer is "the lifting of the mind and heart to God." This definition suggests that when we pray we turn both our intellects and our wills to God. Our thoughts and our love are offered as gifts to the Lord God. In a very real sense we offer ourselves when we pray.

Writers on spirituality remind us that prayer is less what we do and give to the Lord than what God does and gives to us. We are capable of prayer because our Father encourages us to pray. God is always present to us. He and his Son Jesus have already given us the Holy Spirit who dwells within us and prompts us to meet God and to let his love touch us. He has made us a gift.

We can also think of prayer as "*opening* our minds and hearts to God." Openness is the attitude we should have when we turn to God in prayer. We express openness when we listen for God speaking in our hearts and when we acknowledge his love. We can expect to enjoy our meetings with the Lord just as we enjoy time spent with a trusted and valued friend. And even when we do not feel the Lord's nearness, we know that he is closer to us than we are to ourselves. His love is deep within us and will transform us. God loves us, and that fundamental fact will never change.

As we begin to pray, then, we can think of ourselves as gifts, gifts which the Lord has already accepted. As we turn our minds and hearts toward God we may want to respond to his presence with the words of the prophet Isaiah, "Here I am, Lord."

Time to Pray

Availability, both exterior and interior, is a major sign of friendship. Exterior availability means making time to be with a friend. Interior availability, on the other hand, is being truly aware of the friend when we are with the person. Interior availability means listening.

If we are sincere in our efforts to meet the Lord in prayer, we need to set aside time. Ten minutes a day is a good start for a beginner in prayer; 20 minutes is better. But five minutes is better than nothing at all.

A regular time is most helpful. Many people pray in the morning, but others pray during the noon meal break, during the quiet time before dinner, or before going to sleep at night. There may be a special time during commuting to or from work. Any time is a good time for prayer, but we need to be committed to the time we select. This is time we have set aside for a very special friend, not just "extra" time stolen from a busy schedule.

It is wise not to select a time right after a big meal or following strenuous exercise. We need a time when we are at rest and unlikely to be interrupted, a time when we are free from tiredness and daily concerns.

A Place to Pray

Just as important as a regular time to pray is a special place to pray. Since Jesus came into the world, every place is holy. We can pray anywhere.

Jesus himself prayed in many different places. He prayed in the synagogues on Saturday. He prayed before and after meals. He withdrew to the desert, climbed mountains, went to a beautiful garden, walked beside the seashore and found other places to be alone and pray. He offered prayer during the Last Supper. He even uttered prayers from the cross.

The modern spiritual master Charles de Foucauld prayed in the desert. The ancient saint Simon the Stylite climbed a 60-foot pillar and prayed and taught from there for 36 years.

I have three favorite places to pray. One is my den, a hideaway where I do my schoolwork and my writing. It is a cozy room with shelves for my favorite books. In the wall space not allotted to books hang maps; pictures painted by my students and given to me as presents; a picture of my championship golf team from my coaching days; posters of beautiful scenes; a family genealogy, coat of arms and a portrait of an ancient ancestor; and religious pictures and icons. Various versions of the Bible are within easy reach. The book shelves include a generous sampling of spiritual books. Everything I need for prayer and meditation, for the inward journey, is in this room. But the best feature of the room is that it has a door—a door that can be shut whenever I want to work, to read or to pray.

I also pray in my car. After driving to and from the same work location for many years, I can almost do it in my sleep (and, truth to tell, I sometimes think I do). When I am not driving students back and forth to school, I'll carry on a conversation with the Lord, imagining him seated to my right. He's heard an awful lot over the years by occupying the seat next to me.

My third favorite place to pray is outside. When I am praying over a decision, I seem to do it much better while I am walking. I have found that a walk with the Lord refreshes me and helps me think more clearly.

We all find places that are special to us, that facilitate our prayer. The important thing is not so much where we pray or even how we pray but that we pray. Jesus did give us wise advice, though, when he taught us to withdraw to our rooms to pray. Finding a place to pray in our room or in a special corner of the house has a number of advantages. First, we can create a prayerful atmosphere. We may choose to hang a crucifix or icon on the wall to help us fix our attention during prayer. Or we may keep our bible or other books of spiritual reading in the area. Some find lighting a candle or burning incense conducive to prayer. All of these aids to prayer can help us withdraw from our everyday concerns and focus our attention on the Lord's presence.

A second advantage of having a private place to pray is that it can help us relax and be ourselves. We might want to pray lying down or seated in a lotus position. No one but the Lord is there to see us or hear what we have to say. We have the freedom to be spontaneous, to cry if we want, to whisper, to sing.

Prayer Posture

If we can pray anywhere, we can also pray in any position. Sometimes we have to experiment to discover the prayer posture that works best for us. We may adapt the position to the place where we find ourselves in prayer. For example, if we are outside, *walking* may be the best position for this prayer time. If we find ourselves by a lake or a gently flowing stream, we might *sit* on the sandy beach or the warm earth and become part of the symphony of God's creation, thanking him for the beauty he created.

Here are some popular positions for prayer:

- *Lying down.*   Lie down on the floor on your back. Stretch out your legs, keeping your heels close together. Close your eyes or fix them on the ceiling. You can also lie down on your bed, but there is always the danger that you will become so comfortable that you'll fall asleep.

- *Kneeling.*   Pray-ers often kneel to show that they recognize their dependence on God. It is the prayer posture of humility. Many people find it a good way to pray for short periods of time, especially in church or beside their bed. If you choose this position, keep your back straight and rest your hands on the pew in front of you or on your bed.

- *Sitting.*   One of the most popular prayer postures is sitting down. This is an ideal position because it helps achieve the twin aims of all prayer posture: relaxation and alertness. The goal of any prayer posture is to help the body relax so that the spirit might be free of tension and alert enough to listen to the Lord speaking during the prayer time. Sitting is also ideal for reading the Bible or some other book of spiritual reading.

- *Back in a straight line.*   Many experienced pray-ers note the merits of sitting erect in a straight-backed chair, making sure that their head, neck and back are in a straight line. By not leaning back on the chair itself, a feeling of relaxed alertness can be achieved.

An alternative posture is the lotus position, borrowed from the religious practice of Eastern religions. This position is taken by sitting on the floor with the legs crossed and pulled in toward the body. Keep your back straight and your hands open and relaxed on your lap, palms upward. Fix your eyes either on the wall or on an imaginary spot a few feet in front of you.

The straight-back position tends to relax the body so that prayer time refreshes both body and spirit.

Relaxation

We live in a fast-paced world. Sounds and sights continuously bombard our senses. The radio and TV blare; cars, trucks and planes fill the air with noise. Deadlines are a fact of life for most people, and the clock may rule our lives. As a result of this powerful onslaught of our senses we become tense.

The Lord instructs us to "be still and know that I am God." We cannot pray well unless we slow down and create the proper mental climate. We must first relax and allow the tensions of the day to drain out of our overstimulated spirits and bodies.

Creating a relaxed mood for prayer is the last preliminary to praying—after we have made time, found a place and assumed a comfortable position for our prayer. Here are three popular methods for relaxing before prayer:

• *Awareness of our senses.* Sit on a straight chair. Assume a comfortable position. Close your eyes. Take a deep breath, hold it momentarily, and then let it go. Relax your body. Begin with your neck muscles, then your shoulders, your chest and back, your arms and legs.

Be aware of the clothes on your shoulders, on

your back. Become aware of your legs and buttocks pressing on the chair. Feel your feet on the floor. Notice your posture. Become aware of your hands, how they feel, if they are touching or separate.

Repeat this pattern of awareness: Take a deep breath. Relax the neck muscles, the shoulders, the trunk, the arms and legs. Feel the clothes on your shoulders and back, the press of your legs on the chair. Note your posture. Be aware of your legs, your feet, your hands. Feel the heat or coolness of the room.

Go through the exercise again. Feel the tension drain out of your body. Dwell on the part of your body that is most tense. Relax the forehead, the jaw, the neck. Let your arms and legs rest. Come to total stillness. Now you are ready to pray.

• *Breathing.*   Take a relaxing position, seated or lying down. Let the tension drain from your body. Now focus on your breathing. Observe your breathing. Note how fast or slow it is. Notice the air as it comes in and goes out.

Don't try to control your breathing. Just observe it for a few quiet, peaceful moments. Be aware of how it comes in to fill your lungs, and how it goes out of your nostrils.

After a short time spent observing your breathing, begin to count your breaths silently. Count "one" as you inhale; "and" as you exhale. Count "two" as you breathe in again; "and" on the exhalation. Continue your count to 15 or 20.

Now that you are relaxed and aware, try the following breathing meditation:

> Think of the air as an immense ocean filled with God's presence. You are like a fish in this ocean surrounded by the peace and love of God.

Feel the warmth of this ocean of love around you.

Now turn to your prayer. Imagine that every time you take in a breath you are drawing in the peace, love and power of God. Stay with this awareness. Enjoy it.

When you breathe out, imagine that you are exhaling all your fears, your bad attitudes, your negative thoughts.

Imagine as you breathe in God's life and love that you are becoming alive with God's power and love. Imagine as you breathe out that you are ridding yourself of all that is keeping you from being radiantly alive with God's love.

Stay with this prayer for ten minutes or so if you can.

• *Listening.*   Take a comfortable position. Close your eyes. Relax the tension in your body. Feel the tightness drain from your face, your neck, your shoulders, your arms and legs.

Feel the air on your skin. Be aware of each breath that you take in and let out.

Block your ears with your thumbs. Listen to each breath as you take it in and let it out.

After ten breaths, let your hands rest on your lap. Now be attentive to all the sounds around you. Hear them all, the ones close to you and the ones in the background, the big sounds and the little noises.

After a bit, listen to the sounds blend together. Let them penetrate you. Continue with this until you are at rest and ready to turn to prayer.

Distractions in Prayer

The purpose of finding an acceptable time and a quiet place to pray as well as settling into a comfortable position and coming to a state of relaxed alertness is simply to enable us to come into God's presence. These preliminaries to prayer should enable us to open up to God so that we can enter into conversation—talking and listening.

But even after these preliminaries are taken care of, there is still the problem of distractions. Just when we are ready to meet the Lord, thoughts sometimes flood our minds. We find ourselves reliving the events of the day—a tense situation at work, what we *should* have said when we were unjustly criticized, a medical worry, a bill we forgot to pay. We are suddenly in the midst of creating a lesson plan for tomorrow's class, a menu for the week's meals, an estate plan for a client. Perhaps feelings intrude into our prayer time. We find that we have an itch to scratch, or we feel anger at a hurt or slight that comes to mind, or we anticipate something we are going to do later in the day.

Bothersome distractions will inevitably come our way no matter how well we have prepared for our time with the Lord. But how do we deal with them?

• Remember that prayer can happen even if you don't "feel" anything going on. *Wanting* to pray is itself a prayer. Contemporary spiritual writer Father Henri Nouwen has some wise words to say about this common experience:

> One of the experiences of prayer is that it seems that nothing happens. But when you stay with it and look back over a long period of prayer, you suddenly realize that something has happened. What is most close, most intimate, most present, often cannot be experienced directly but only with a certain distance. When I think that I am only distracted, just wasting my time, something is happening too immediate for knowing, understanding, and experiencing. Only in retrospect do I realize that something very important has happened. Isn't this true of all really important

events in life? When I am together with someone I love very much, we seldom talk about our
relationship. The relationship, in fact, is too central to be a subject of talk. . . . When I pray, my
prayer often seems very confused, dull, uninspir-
ing, and distracted. God is close but often too
close to experience. God is nearer to me than I
am to myself and, therefore, no subject for feelings or thoughts.[1]

Keep reminding yourself that God is present to you.

• Be patient with yourself. After taking care of the
preliminaries, don't rush the Lord. Almost anything
we try to do to make us feel God's presence is probably wrong. The Lord will lead you in his good time.

• Focusing on a religious picture, an icon or a crucifix may help you keep your attention on meeting
God. An icon, for example, is often called "a meeting
between heaven and earth." The spiritual idea behind
using an icon or other religious art in prayer is that it
helps to provide a line of communication between the
person praying and the holy image portrayed in the
art.

Find an icon like the famous "Our Lady of Perpetual Help." Prayerfully place yourself before the
icon. Study the symbolism: the archangels Michael
and Gabriel carrying the instruments of the crucifixion; the gold background which represents heaven;
the Virgin Mary who gives her Son to the world; the
infant Jesus who looks out into the world and the
mission of salvation he has been sent to accomplish.
Place yourself in the scene. Allow the picture and its
message to speak to you.

• Ask the Holy Spirit, who lives within, to guide

---

[1] Henri J. M. Nouwen, *The Genesee Diary: Report From a Trappist Monastery* (Garden City, New York: Doubleday & Company, Inc., Image Books,
1976), pp. 140-141.

you in your prayer time. You might also pray to a favorite saint to intercede on your behalf.

• Don't try to resist distracting thoughts. Let them happen. Then try to control them by one of these methods:

Make sure you are relaxed. Picture your thoughts as bubbles rising to the surface of a small pond. Every thought is a different bubble. Watch the thoughts rise, burst and disappear. Try to clear the pond of all the bubbles/thoughts. Picture a clear, calm surface on the pond. Come to peace and return to the presence of the Lord.

Or observe your thoughts. Imagine yourself sitting by a gently flowing river. You sit and watch. Imagine your distractions to be logs which float in front of you. Let the river current carry the logs away. Observe the logs go by, but don't follow them. After a time, all the logs will float by, and you will have cleared your mind. Come to peace and return to the Lord.

A Prayer Reflection

Find a quiet place to pray. Assume a comfortable position and use one of the relaxation exercises.

Now close your eyes. Imagine you are entering a dark and quiet tunnel. There are no sights or sounds in this tunnel. You are alert, but very relaxed and quiet.

You see yourself traveling deeper into the tunnel. It is very quiet. You do see a light at the other end though. At first it is just a tiny dot, but it slowly gets larger. You sense yourself getting closer and closer to the light.

When you reach the end of the tunnel, you enter into a bright, warm, peaceful light. You are enveloped in the light. You feel its warmth and are dazzled by its glow. Slowly, the image of Jesus comes into view. He has a smile on his face. His eyes are looking at you. Study his face. Look at his love and warmth and acceptance. Let his total love of you penetrate your being. Feel his love touch your heart. Deeply sense the joy he has for you.

Allow the Lord to look at you. He does so lovingly and humbly. Enjoy his peaceful gaze and the love he showers on you.

Thank the Lord for all he has given you.

A Scripture Reflection

"When you pray, go to your private room, shut yourself in, and so pray to your Father who is in that secret place, and your Father who sees all that is done in secret will reward you" (Mt 6:6).

3
Learning to Pray With Jesus

How does a person learn to pray? Those who are new to the prayer journey would be wise to seek out a trusty guide to show the way. Even those who have been praying for a while can greatly profit from looking at "old ground" with a fresh eye.

We see the value of a guide in many human endeavors. One of my passions in life is the game of golf. To me there is nothing so relaxing as a day on the links with some good friends. The beauty of well-manicured fairways, the camaraderie, the challenge inherent in the game—all help me to relax and escape the cares and stresses of my everyday routine.

But I am a self-taught player. I have a horrible swing— an amusing loop-the-loop—that my golfing buddies delight in poking fun at. Bad habits have crept into my swing and are ingrained in my muscle memory. I have learned to play with this swing, but I know its deficiencies only too well.

I regret not having learned to play properly when I was younger. Only in recent years have I finally gained the proper amount of humility to ask for and learn from seasoned golfers who know how to teach the mechanics of the game. There is no substitute for the guidance of a good teacher.

The same is also true in the prayer life. Novices—indeed all those who wish to become better pray-ers—can always benefit from a guide. And the best, the most dependable, is Jesus himself, the Son who is the Way to the Father.

What does Jesus teach us about prayer? When we turn to the gospels to answer that question, we become aware that prayer was very important in Jesus' own life. From him we learn how to pray; he not only gave us the great prayer, the Our Father, but he showed us by his life how we should approach God in prayer. Like any good guide, he backed up his words with his own example.

Jesus at Prayer

After being baptized in the Jordan River, Jesus made a 40-day retreat in the desert before launching his public ministry. Prayer was the preparation Jesus chose for a crucial period in his life. Jesus also prayed before making a decision. He prayed the whole night before selecting his apostles, the men who would have a special role in carrying on his work after his earthly ministry was over. He prayed over his impending death on the cross. The content of this prayer is significant. Jesus, like us, experienced fear at the thought of death. Yet he prayed:

> "Father," he said, "if you are willing, take this cup away from me. Nevertheless, let your will be done, not mine" (Lk 22:42).

Jesus did not hesitate to ask for what he wanted—a way out of the death in store for him—but his prayer was one not only of petition but of submission.

Jesus withdrew often to lonely places to pray. He liked to pray on hills, as he did after the miracle of the loaves and fishes when he dismissed the crowd and his disciples and withdrew to a hill to pray. He also prayed on mountains, one time in the presence of Peter, James and John at the time of his transfiguration.

Jesus offered prayers of praise, thanksgiving and petition, thus teaching us how to approach his Father. Jesus *praised* the Father for revealing his will to the humble and lowly:

> Just at this time, filled with joy by the Holy Spirit, he said, "I bless you, Father, Lord of heaven and earth, for hiding these things from the learned and the clever and revealing them to little children" (Lk 10:21).

Jesus also *thanked* God when he raised Lazarus from the dead:

> "Father, I thank you for hearing my prayer.
> I myself knew that you hear me always,
> but I speak
> for the sake of all these who are standing around me,
> so that they may believe it was you who sent me" (Jn 11:41-42).

As we so often do, Jesus *petitioned* God for many things. He prayed that Simon Peter not be tempted. In his great priestly prayer of intercession (Chapter 17 of John's gospel), Jesus remembered all those who have been entrusted to him that they may remain in truth. We can take great comfort in knowing that Jesus prays for us.

Luke tells us that Jesus, like all good Jews of his time, prayed every Saturday in the synagogue. Scripture also reveals that Jesus celebrated the various religious festivals so important to Jewish worship. As a good Jew, Jesus would have prayed in the morning when rising, at noon, and in the evening before retiring. He would also have recited prayers before and after eating his meals.

Jesus knew the Jewish scriptures well and often prayed the psalms. He sang psalms with the apostles after the Last

Supper on the way to the Garden of Gethsemane, and he recited Psalm 22 on the cross:

> *"Eloi, eloi, lama sabachthani?"* which means, *"My God, my God, why have you forsaken me?"* (Mk 15:34).

Jesus prayed as he hung on the cross dying. He prayed for sinners. He forgave those who put him to death. He died surrendering himself in trust to God:

> "Father, *into your hands I commit my spirit*" (Lk 23:46).

Jesus' life and death dramatically testified that prayer was vital to him. It kept him close to his Father and helped him live a life of service for us, his brothers and sisters. To live a life in ever-deepening relationship to God and in service to our fellow human beings, we too must pray.

Jesus' Teaching on Prayer

Jesus offers us wise advice on how to pray. We saw before that Jesus advised us to go to our rooms to pray. A quiet place has two advantages for private prayer. First, it gets us away from the distractions of our busy day so we can peacefully spend time with God. Second, it purifies our motives. When we are away from others, we won't give in to the temptation to think about how we appear to them. Jesus had little patience with those who prayed so they would appear holy to others. The right intention in prayer is vitally important to the Lord.

Jesus also taught the following things about prayer.

• *Keep your prayer short.*   Heaping up a lot of words does not make our prayer more effective. Jesus taught us to keep our prayers short and to the point:

> "In your prayers do not babble as the gentiles do, for they think that by using many words they will make themselves heard. Do not be like them; your Father knows what you need before you ask him" (Mt 6:7-8).

• *Pray with childlike simplicity.*   Jesus taught us to pray as little children do. He reminded us that God's love far surpasses any earthly love we may have experienced.

> "What father among you, if his son asked for a fish, would hand him a snake? Or if he asked for an egg, hand him a scorpion? If you then, evil as you are, know how to give your children what is good, how much more will the heavenly Father give the Holy Spirit to those who ask him!" (Lk 11:11-13).

God always hears our petitions, and he will always give us what is good for us.

• *Pray with faith.*   In Matthew's gospel Jesus instructs us to be confident when we pray:

> "In truth I tell you, if you have faith and do not doubt at all, not only will you do what I have done to the fig tree, but even if you say to this mountain, 'Be pulled up and thrown into the sea,' it will be done. And if you have faith, everything you ask for in prayer, you will receive" (Mt 21:21-22).

• *Be persistent.*   Jesus also tells us not to lose heart, but to persist in prayer. In Luke 11:5-8 Jesus tells the delightful story of a person who is visited by his friend at the ungodly hour of midnight. He has nothing in the house to offer his late-night visitor, so he goes next door to his neighbor's house to request some bread for his guest. The neighbor is already in bed and doesn't want to get up for fear that he'll awaken the children. But Jesus says if the neighbor won't get up out of friendship, he will if his friend keeps knocking on the door!

• *Pray with others.*   Jesus encourages prayer with others as well as private prayer; for example, he instructs us to celebrate the Eucharist with others in his name. He also teaches that there is great value in joining our prayers with those of others:

> "In truth I tell you once again, if two of you on earth agree to ask anything at all, it will be granted to you by my Father in heaven. For where two or three meet in my name, I am there among them" (Mt 18:19-20).

• *Pray with a forgiving heart.*   Finally, Jesus instructs us to pray with a forgiving heart. He doesn't want us to approach God full of anger and hate. He wants a calm heart and loving spirit in us when we approach our Father in prayer:

> "And when you stand in prayer, forgive whatever you have against anybody, so that your Father in heaven may forgive your failings too" (Mk 11:25).

It is perhaps this last lesson that is the hardest for us to learn. When we have been hurt, we tend to store up our pain and our anger. We find prayer difficult, and the thought of praying *for* the one who has harmed us is distasteful. Yet that is precisely what we are called to do.

It is not easy. When my wife and I have a squabble, my inclination is to blame her, to seethe in resentment, and to wait for her to apologize. I don't want to pray for her. Yet in praying I often discover that the source of my hurt is as much my fault as it is hers. Asking the Lord to heal us has typically shown me that my own self-righteousness has added to the friction between us.

And I find it best not to wait to forgive a person who has harmed me (either in reality or in my imagination). The passage of time too often breeds resentment, especially with someone close. I have made it a rule not to go to bed angry with my wife. (On rare occasions we have been up as late as 4 a.m.!) But this rule has helped us weather some of the storms that have inevitably come our way over the years. We need to be humble enough to ask for forgiveness and gracious enough to extend it freely and ungrudgingly.

How do we go about praying for someone who has hurt us? The following steps may lead to a sincere prayer of love and forgiveness:

1. Ask yourself if you really want to forgive the other person. Is your attitude, "I can forgive, but I cannot forget" or "I want to forgive, but I can't"? Are you saying, "I don't really want to forgive" or "Maybe I'll be able to forgive later, but not yet"?

2. Examine your resentment. Get your feelings toward the other person out in the open. Imagine that the other person is standing in front of you. Tell him or her why you are hurting inside.

3. Now look at the situation from the other person's point of view. Did you perhaps contribute to the painful situation. Might the other person be hurting too? Do you feel any compassion for the other person?

4. Finally, put yourself in the presence of the Lord. See him on the cross. Picture yourself and the person who has hurt you standing below the cross. See Jesus looking at both of you. Hear him speak words of forgiveness both to the person whom you resent *and* to you. See the Lord loving the other person. Ask him to help you love this person too. Ask him to give you the strength to forgive. Stay with this scene until you feel some of your anger begin to slip away. The Lord loves both you and the person who has hurt you. He forgives both of you. Can you forgive too?

The Perfect Prayer: The Our Father

The Our Father, the Lord's Prayer, holds the preeminent position among all Christian prayers. From the earliest centuries until today, the Lord's Prayer has been used in the liturgy of the church—in all the sacraments and especially in the Eucharist. We have made it part of our daily prayer. We recite it on special occasions, and whenever we gather to pray.

Background

Both Luke and Matthew record the Lord's Prayer, though they place the prayer in different settings. Their wording is also slightly different:

Our Father in heaven	Father,
may your name be held holy	may your name be held holy,
your kingdom come,	your kingdom come;
your will be done,	
on earth as in heaven.	
Give us today our daily bread.	give us each day our daily bread,
And forgive us our debts,	and forgive us our sins,
as we have forgiven those who are in debt to us.	for we ourselves forgive each one who is in debt to us.
And do not put us to the test, but save us from the Evil One (Mt 6:9-13).	And do not put us to the test (Lk 11:2-4).

Luke's version of the Lord's Prayer has only five petitions while Matthew's has seven. Scholars believe that Luke's is probably the older version and is thus closer to the actual words of Jesus. Matthew's version, the one we are most familiar with, was used in liturgies of baptism and the Eucharist in the early church. The conclusion we add at Mass, "for thine is the kingdom, the power and the glory forever and ever, Amen," first appeared in the *Didache*, an early manual of catechetical instruction which dates from the first century.

Matthew has Jesus teaching the Our Father as part of the Sermon on the Mount (Mt 5-7). In the Sermon on the Mount Jesus teaches his followers a way to live which is consistent with the coming of the kingdom of God. We, the disciples of Jesus, should not pray to show off; nor should we babble so that we may be heard. We are to pray the simple prayer Jesus taught, the prayer that contains the good news in miniature, the Our Father.

In Luke's gospel Jesus is praying in a quiet place when the apostles come and ask him to teach them to pray "as John taught his disciples" (Lk 11:1). Jesus then teaches them the Our Father. In Luke's gospel Jesus gives his followers a formula, a way to pray that marks them as belonging especially to him. The Our Father gives them—and us—an identity; it sets us off as special children who are privileged to address God as *Abba*. That intimate term, *Abba*, is a form of address no one would have dared to use for the almighty God before Jesus invited us to do so. The Lord's Prayer was not taught to early Christians until the week after they were baptized. It was the prayer of *Christian* identity.

Reflective Praying

A good method of praying is to take any prayer, like the Our Father, and slowly reflect on each word or phrase in it. Let us now turn to the phrases of the Our Father using this method as we take a closer look at what Jesus taught us.

• *Our Father who art in heaven.*   Jesus invites us to call God *Abba,* to address the almighty God intimately, securely and with childlike trust. Jesus teaches us that God is a good, gracious and absolutely loving parent.

Jesus' invitation to call God *Abba* implies two very important truths. First, Jesus' Father is our Father too. He has adopted us. Jesus is our brother. Second, God is *our* Father. We are brothers and sisters to one another; every person is intimately related to us. If we believe what Jesus teaches us by this prayer, we commit ourselves to understand, to love, and to respond to *everyone* who comes into our lives.

> —At work, whom do I need to see more as my brother and sister?

> —In my daily routine is there anybody I relate to only by his or her function, such as the clerk at the store? How can I better relate to this person as a brother or sister?

> —Do I really believe I am God's special child?

• *Hallowed be thy name.*   Each person's name calls forth his or her uniqueness. For many in the ancient world, the name of the person *was* the person. Jesus wanted Simon bar Jonah to be the leader of the apostles, so he renamed him *Peter* which means "rock"; Peter was to be the solid foundation on which Christ would build his community. Our personal names carry meanings too: David is "beloved," Jennifer is "gentle spirit," Christopher means "Christ bearer," Carol is "joyful song."

When we pray for the "hallowing" of God's name, we pray that our Father may be regarded as holy by all people on earth (as he is in heaven). God is the source of all holiness, of all that is good, of all love. We make God's name holy when we believe in his love and act on it by taking on the identity of his Son Jesus. When we live up to the name *Christian*, people will know and praise God because they can see him reflected in us.

> —Am I proud that I bear the name *Christian*?

> —What have I done in the past week to witness to my faith?

• *Thy kingdom come; thy will be done on earth as it is in heaven.*   With the coming of Jesus Christ, God's rule—which is firmly established in heaven—has broken into our world. Peace, justice, truth, community and mutual love reign in heaven. Jesus has inaugurated this

reign through his own ministry. He preached the good
news to the poor, brought liberty to captives, wholeness to
those who were broken, and healing and salvation to all
people.

God's kingdom will be fully established only at the
end of time, but we are to live, experience and work for it
right now. It is God's will that his reign of peace and
justice, of truth and service, be advanced in our world. To
pray for the coming of this kingdom means to join Jesus in
his work: to feed the hungry and give drink to the thirsty,
to welcome the stranger, to clothe the naked, to visit the
sick and the imprisoned, to respond to the needs of all
those who come into our lives, especially those Jesus
called "the least of these."

To do God's will is to love God above all things and
our neighbor as ourselves. Our model, as always, is Jesus.

> —Am I involved in some way with one of the
> great social issues of the day, for example, the
> pro-life movement or the peace movement?

> —Or am I actively engaged in some other way in
> living the corporal works of mercy?

• *Give us this day our daily bread.*   Bread
represents what is needed to sustain life. It also suggests a
meal and the companionship which comes with a meal.
When we pray for our daily bread, we are praying for a
number of things. We are praying for the necessities for
physical life—food, shelter, clothing; psychological
life—friendship, love, companionship; and spiritual
life—Jesus in the Eucharist.

When we pray for *our* bread, we are praying not only
for our own needs but for the needs of all our brothers and
sisters throughout the world. If we mean what we are
saying in our prayer, we become conscious of our
obligation, in justice and love, to share with others,
especially those who are less fortunate.

The word for "daily" in the original Aramaic spoken by Jesus may have also meant something like "for tomorrow, today." When we pray for our daily bread, we are praying for the fullness of God's material and spiritual gifts which will be ours in heaven. We dare to ask God to give us a taste of these gifts today.

> —Do I sacrifice for the poor of the world, cutting back on my consumption and donating time and/or money to those who are in need?

> —What is my attitude toward the Eucharist? Might I participate in the Mass an extra day sometime during the coming week?

• *And forgive us our trespasses as we forgive those who trespass against us.* As we said before, it is difficult for most of us to forgive those who have hurt us. It is also difficult, perhaps even more so, to ask for forgiveness. But when we ask God for forgiveness, we are honest about ourselves. We admit that we are sinners and in need of God's saving love. We acknowledge that we need Jesus who will help us turn from our selfish ways to a more loving life of service. We confess that we need help on our journey to the Father.

But we must also forgive others. Jesus connects God's forgiveness of us to our forgiveness of others. God's forgiving love should become flesh in our lives as we extend forgiveness to others. When we forgive those who have hurt us, we are communicating love and understanding, thus encouraging them to respond to us in love. The Our Father is a prayer that calls for action: to forgive as we have been forgiven.

> —Is there someone who needs my forgiveness? Could I do something concrete to extend my forgiveness in the immediate future?

—When did I last celebrate the Lord's forgiveness in the sacrament of reconciliation?

• *And lead us not into temptation.*   In following the Lord, trials will come our way. To follow Jesus means to pick up a cross, to endure some suffering in doing the right thing, to pay the price of love. What we pray for in this petition is that we have the strength to overcome any difficulties that might steer us away from a Christian life of service. It also calls us to remove the temptations that keep other people from knowing God: the conditions which keep people impoverished, the culture which encourages pornography and reduces people to objects, the laws which permit the taking of innocent human life, the policies which squander limited resources on destructive weapons that can reduce humanity and our planet to a shambles.

> —What am I doing right now to build up my spiritual strength so that I can resist better any temptation that might come my way?
>
> —Do I deny myself some good thing or some good times for the benefit of some worthy cause?
>
> —Is there any sacrifice in my life?

• *But deliver us from evil.*   Finally, we pray that we might be delivered from the snares of Satan and a sensuous, materialistic and violent society which ignores God and tempts us to rely on ourselves. We pray that God may spare us from the evil of accidents, illness and natural disasters. We pray that God will strengthen us to confront the evil for which we too share some blame—exploiting others, injustice, prejudice. Lastly, we pray that we never be put in the situation where we might be tempted to deny our loving Creator. This would be the greatest evil of all.

> —Is there something in my life that is keeping

me from loving God above all things and my neighbor as myself?

—Have I asked the Lord to free me from bondage to this inordinate attraction?

A Prayer Reflection

Reflection can help us evaluate the progress we are making on our spiritual journey. St. Ignatius of Loyola taught the following technique:

Step 1: Focusing

Begin by using one of the relaxation techniques that you find effective.

Be aware of God's loving presence. Think of the gifts he has granted you during this past day. Thank him for these gifts.

Step 2: Insight

Ask the Holy Spirit to enlighten both your mind and heart and to help you to appreciate that you are a child of a loving and generous Creator.

Step 3: Evaluation

Now look at your life this past day in the light of the life and teaching of Jesus. Ask yourself these questions:

- What thoughts, words and actions of this past day conformed best to the life modelled by Jesus?

- What thoughts, words and actions of this past day reflected a failure to love as Jesus loved?

- How can I improve tomorrow?

Step 4: Forgiveness

Ask God to touch you and forgive your failings of the past day. Promise to do better tomorrow.

Step 5: Thanksgiving

Thank the Creator, Son and Spirit for being with you and helping you to be honest. Thank the Triune God for the gift of life, the gift of honesty about yourself and the gift of God's deep love for you.

This examination of conscience is best done at the end of the day in the quiet hours when we are alone with ourselves and our God.

A Scripture Reflection

As you sent me into the world,
I have sent them into the world,
and for their sake I consecrate myself
so that they too may be consecrated in truth.
I pray not only for these
but also for those
who through their teaching will come to believe in me.
May they all be one,
just as, Father, you are in me and I am in you,
so that they also may be in us,
so that the world may believe it was you who sent me
    (Jn 17:18-21).

4
Meditation and Contemplation

Forty years ago General Omar Bradley, then chairman of the Joint Chiefs of Staff, sagely observed:

> We have too many men of science, too few men of God. We have grasped the mystery of the atom and rejected the Sermon on the Mount. Ours is a world of nuclear giants and ethical infants. We know more about war than we know about peace, more about killing than we know about living.[1]

These prophetic words are as true today as they were at the threshold of the Cold War. But from time to time God raises up men and women who show us by their lives the meaning of peace. A remarkable film of our decade, *Gandhi*, depicted the life and witness of one such man, the Mahatma or Great Soul. Many people who saw this film were struck by the spiritual power of Gandhi and his Hindu religion. Although Gandhi rejected Christianity, he embraced Jesus Christ and taught Christians everywhere that Jesus' message of peace is a practical message for 20th-century people.

Because of "great souls" like Mohandas K. Gandhi, Western society has begun to discover the spiritual message

---

[1] Quoted in Louis Fischer, *Gandhi: His Life and Message for the World* (New York: New American Library, 1954), p. 133.

49

and power of the great Eastern religions. In addition to the witness of Gandhi's life, popular gurus from India teach relaxation techniques like Transcendental Meditation (TM), saffron-robed devotees of the Hindu god Krishna proffer flowers at our busy airports, and perceptive authors write books in which they apply Eastern techniques of concentration to enhance performance in sports. All of these call our attention to another way of doing things.

Many spiritual writers in our Catholic tradition—Trappist Thomas Merton and Jesuit William Johnston among others—have also taught us that we have much to learn from the spiritual treasures which can be found in the religions of the East. One benefit of turning to the East has been a renewed appreciation for the rich prayer tradition of meditation and contemplation in Christianity itself, a tradition that has been around from the earliest centuries of our religion.

Meditation and contemplation aim to bring about communion with God. Many Christians who practice meditation and contemplation discover a new vitality and growth in their spiritual lives, not the least of which is the kind of peace and joy that come from the realization that all life is sacred because it participates in God's creative goodness. This is the very insight that animated Gandhi's vision and that of so many others who practice the spiritual disciplines of the great religions of the East.

Here we will discuss meditation and contemplation, paths of prayer common to both Christianity and many other religions of the world. Our discussion will suggest several ways to meditate and introduce the Jesus Prayer as a guide to contemplative prayer.

A brief definition of each of these two kinds of prayer is in order. *Meditation* is a "tuning in to God," thinking about God and trying to become aware of the divine presence all around us and its action in our lives. Meditation typically involves active use of the mind and imagination. It requires being attentive to the many ways the Lord might be revealing himself to us. For example, we are meditating when we think about our spouse or closest friend and what he or she means to us. When we reflect on what a wonderful gift this person is, when we ask the Lord to show us what he is saying through this person, when we thank God for this very special individual, then we are meditating.

Contemplation, on the other hand, is much more passive. When we contemplate, we are not actively "tuning in to God"; rather, we are simply sitting in God's presence. Spiritual writer Carlo Carretto describes contemplation this way:

> To be watched by God: that is how I would define contemplation, which is passive rather than active, more a matter of silence than of words, of waiting rather than action.[2]

Contemplation, then, is like sitting on the seashore and enjoying a spectacular sunset. It isn't necessary to say or even think anything. We are just there, present to the beauty, enjoying it. In contemplative prayer we simply enjoy being with the Lord; we don't have to *do* anything at all.

LEARNING TO MEDITATE

The dictionary defines *meditate* this way: "to reflect upon, to ponder; to plan or intend in the mind." These definitions are good because they emphasize that meditation is a form of mental prayer; the activity of the prayer takes place in the mind.

Meditation is natural for human beings. Notice a baby looking out at its world. The infant studies the faces of its parents, looks with excitement on its toys, absorbs and internalizes every sensation that comes its way.

Meditation continues as we grow older. We sometimes

---

[2] Carlo Carretto, *In Search of the Beyond* (Maryknoll, New York: Orbis Books, 1976), p. 79.

find ourselves, at least occasionally, reflecting deeply on some things that are very important to us. As teen-agers we tried to imagine our futures—what kind of person we might marry, whether we were being called to religious life, what our place in the world might be. In mid-life we reflect on our worldly and spiritual journey thus far and plan for the future. In old age we gather up the ends of our journey and seek new perspectives on the transition to new life that awaits us. At any stage we may be confronted by pain and suffering, intense joy, unexpected loss. If we reflect on these intense experiences, we grow in under-standing.

Meditation requires a certain degree of discipline, imagination and attentiveness to what is taking place in our lives. The following characteristics are typical of a person who has developed good background skills for meditation:

He or she is . . .

- a good listener
- in touch with his or her feelings
- sensitive to the feelings of others
- capable of enjoying the simple things in life
- perceptive enough to see many implications in most situations
- capable of dreaming about what could be rather than always accepting what is
- in touch with God

We can meditate about anything and everything, but in learning to meditate it is usually good to start with some simple object or scene. We can think about it carefully, and then ponder what it is saying to us.

Meditation becomes prayerful when its focus is on the Lord and what he might be saying to us in our lives. Christian meditation has a long, rich history. Many great saints have taught us good ways to focus our attention on God and have suggested techniques that help to draw us closer to God. This history begins with the desert Fathers. Down through the centuries saints like St. Benedict of Nursia, St. Gregory of Sinai, the unknown author of *The Cloud of Unknowing*, St. Ignatius of Loyola, St. Teresa of Avila, St. John of the Cross and St. Francis de Sales have taught us valuable ways to meditate. In our own day, mystical writers like Charles de Foucauld, Pierre Teilhard de Chardin and Thomas Merton have kept alive the Christian tradition of meditation.

Meditating on a Simple Object

A good way to begin to learn and to practice meditation is to follow a very simple procedure such as the following.

Preliminaries:

First, select a common object from nature on which to meditate. Here are some ideas: weeds and grasses, leaves, flowers, stones, small shells, twigs, seed pods, pine cones, small vegetables.

Next, find a place with a minimum of exterior distractions. Assume a comfortable position. Inhale and exhale slowly, being aware of the air coming in and going out. Close your eyes and listen to the sounds around you. Be at peace, quiet and still.

Steps in the Meditation:

1. Observe.   The first step in a simple meditation is to observe carefully the object you have chosen. In this stage you want to know everything there is to know about the object. Suppose you chose an acorn. Feel its smooth texture. Notice its colors, its form, its shape. Put it to your lips. Smell it. Feel its texture next to your cheek. Place it by your ear. Touch your tongue to it or stroke it very gently with your fingertips. Try to capture the feeling a child would have encountering an acorn for the first time. Learn all you can about it. (Usually you will only spend about five minutes on this phase of the meditation.)

2. Reflect.   Ask yourself the question, What does this mean? Make full use of your imagination in this phase of the meditation. Close your eyes. Ask the acorn what it is saying to you. You might think for a while of the tall oak tree that dropped it to the ground. Or perhaps you will picture it being squirreled away to provide a nutritious meal for some small animal during the winter. Or you could see the little oak seed taking root and gradually growing into a tall, sturdy tree. Perhaps you can feel the power and mystery of life hidden in the small acorn you are holding. It is a little repository of potential life which, if properly planted and nourished, will unleash tremendous power. Perhaps you will imagine the thousands of acorns that could come from this one little acorn, the other trees they might create, the shade these trees will give, the safety their branches will provide for the birds, and so on. What is it that is so very special about this particular object which God has made? (Spend another five minutes or so imagining what your object means.)

3. Listen.   Meditation is a way to listen to God. But so far you haven't even consciously thought of God. Now, in this stage of the meditation, turn to the Creator to see what the message of this wonderful object might be. Select a couple of your observations and see if there is a message there for your life. Perhaps you were struck by the fact that an acorn is a powerful little bundle of life that can bring forth great growth. You recognize that you too are like that. God has given you gifts that, if nurtured, can bring forth life in other people. Ask the Lord to show you where your gifts are and how you can nourish them. Make a mental note of whatever insight might come to you and thank God for sharing it with you. (Spend another five minutes listening to what the Lord might be saying to you through the object of your meditation.)

Ending the Meditation, a Resolution:

It is usually a good idea to make some kind of resolution as you conclude the meditation. You might recite a prayer thanking God for any insights he has given you. Perhaps you might thank the Lord for helping you to realize what great potential you have for advancing the kingdom in the world. Or you might praise God for the beautiful things created for our enjoyment which we all too often take for granted. Or if your meditation revealed a bad habit, you might promise the Lord that you will do better, no matter what the cost. By resolving to do something with your meditation, you will be able to relate it to your everyday life. (Two or three minutes may be sufficient for this concluding stage of the meditation.)

The simple object used in the above meditation can easily be a picture. Picture-praying has a rich history in the church. Catholics have used holy cards, picture books, stained-glass windows, icons, paintings, slides and films to help them pray. Taking pictures can also be a form of prayer. Prayer and picture-taking have much in common. Prayer helps us focus on God; photography helps us focus on a created reality. Prayer brings us in union with God; photography helps us capture a scene so we can keep it, at least in some sense. Prayer takes practice; so does good photography.

Meditating with a camera has an added benefit. You can use the results as aids to meditation following the steps outlined above. Here are the steps to a simple meditation using a camera:

1. Obtain a simple-to-operate camera. Use either black-and-white or color film for prints or slides.

2. Reserve about an hour to take a walk outside. (It is easiest to use natural lighting.) Observe carefully everything you see.

3. Choose several subjects to photograph: people, scenes, objects. Natural forms like trees, flowers, ponds and rivers make good subjects. So do people—their expressions, their hands, their eyes.

4. Having selected a subject, carefully and slowly scan it through your camera. When your eye catches something of interest, snap a picture.

Using Scripture to Meditate

Christians believe that the Bible is the living word of God. For this word to speak to us, though, we must read and reflect on it. We must hear what the Lord is saying to us through the particular scripture reading. Meditation uses the mind and the heart to help us hear the word of the Lord. It engages the faculties of thinking and imagination (our minds), the love we have for God (our hearts), and also the resolutions we make to live better Christian lives (our "hands and feet").

St. Ignatius of Loyola also taught an approach to meditating on the scriptures. He deeply believed in the value of fully engaging our imaginations in our reading and reflecting on the meaning to be found in the Bible. One value of his approach is that it keeps distractions to a minimum.

Let us try a guided meditation on a New Testament passage. Note how similar the approach is to the one taken in the previous section.

Preliminaries:

1. Select a text.   Pick a passage before your time for meditation so you don't waste time paging through the bible. Choose a passage or story that seems to speak to you at this time in your life. For this example, we will use Luke 17:11-19.

2. Settle down.   Take a few minutes to settle down in your place of prayer. Sit with your spine straight, keep your feet on the floor, knees slightly apart, hands on your lap, eyes closed. Breathe deeply and slowly. Be aware of the sounds around you. Quiet yourself and be still.

3. Pray to the Holy Spirit.   Put yourself in God's presence. Feel the warmth and the love. As you slowly inhale and exhale, ask the Holy Spirit to help you pray and to hear what the Lord is saying to you.

4. Read the scripture passage slowly and meditatively.

> Now it happened that on the way to Jerusalem he was travelling in the borderlands of Samaria and Galilee. As he entered one of the villages, ten men suffering from a virulent skin-disease came to meet him. They stood some way off and called to him, "Jesus! Master! Take pity on us." When he saw them he said, "Go and show yourselves to the priests." Now as they were going away they were cleansed. Finding himself cured, one of them turned back praising God at the top of his voice and threw himself prostrate at the feet of Jesus and thanked him. The man was a Samaritan. This led Jesus to say, "Were not all ten made clean? The other nine, where are they? It seems that no one has come back to give praise to God except this foreigner." And he said to the man, "Stand up and go on your way. Your faith has saved you" (Lk 17:11-19).

The Meditation:

1. Observe.   Step into the story and become part of it. What is happening? What kind of day is it? Hot? What is the road like? Dusty? Who is with Jesus?

Imagine yourself as one of the disciples travelling with Jesus. You can't wait to get to town to get a drink of water. See the diseased men, the sores on their arms and faces. They cover their faces. Perhaps they ring a bell to warn travellers away. Then, suddenly, you hear them cry out to Jesus. He looks at them. What is his reaction? Does he approach them? What is your reaction? Do you want your friend and teacher Jesus to shy away from them? Are you afraid he will catch their disease? Are you afraid that you will? Listen to his words. What do they mean? Do you think the men will be cured? What is their reaction? How are the other disciples reacting?

Now imagine that you are one of the sick persons. You walk away to go to the priests when suddenly you are cured. What do you do? Do you come back and thank Jesus? If you don't, what do you do? Why?

Now focus on the Samaritan. He grabs Jesus' feet. He cries with joy. He thanks Jesus and praises him. Listen to Jesus' words. Does he sound disappointed with the others who were also cured? What does he mean when he says, "Your faith has saved you"?

2. Reflect.   What does this story mean? Is it about physical sickness or spiritual sickness? Does it focus on the mercy of Jesus, his compassion for the rejected ones? Is it a call to faith? Is it about gratitude? courage? obedience to the word of the Master? What is Luke stressing in this story? What strikes you as the main point?

3. Listen.   What word is being spoken to you in this bible passage? Do you have a spiritual sickness eating away at you that Jesus wants to touch and cure? Do you have the courage to approach Jesus to ask for his help and salvation? Are you willing to listen to his answer, what you need for the cure? Are you weak in faith? Do you need Jesus to strengthen your faith? Or perhaps he is telling you to say thank you for all that you have been given. Will you be like the Samaritan who came back to offer thanks? Or are you like the ones who take their healing for granted? Prayerfully ask, "What, Lord, are you saying *to me* in this reading?"

Resolution:

After spending 15 minutes or so with the Lord in your meditation, resolve to do something about the insights you have gained. Perhaps you will acknowledge that you are a sinner who needs to approach the Lord and ask for his forgiveness. Perhaps you will resolve to thank God for the health he has given you. Perhaps you will think of a person who has done something for you, and you will now take an opportunity to make some gesture of thanks to this person. Whatever your resolution, thank the Lord for the moments he spent with you and for any insights you received.

If you make a regular habit of meditating with the Bible, you will find yourself growing closer to the Lord. When St. Jerome began his life as a monk, he still preferred to read the works of the Latin writers like Cicero, Virgil and Plautus. Once while he was asleep, the story goes, God appeared to him and asked him who he was.

"I am a Christian," Jerome replied.

"You lie," responded God in Jerome's dream. "You are a Ciceronian; for where your treasure is, there is your heart also."

This dream transformed Jerome's life. He resolved to read, study and pray with the Sacred Scriptures. Jerome became a great lover of the Lord when he turned to his bible. All of us—Jerome's brothers and sisters—who commit ourselves to a regular habit of bible meditation will discover the word of God speaking in our hearts. This experience will cause us to grow in love of God and will also transform our lives. The Bible is a steady guidebook on our journey to God.

We can meditate on any passage in scripture. However, the following passages are especially helpful to beginners in meditation. Experienced pray-ers find them conducive to meditation also.

The Young Jesus (Luke 2:41-50)
Temptation in the Desert (Mt 4:1-11)
Calling of the First Disciples (Lk 5:1-11)
Calming of the Storm (Mk 4:35-41)
The Woman in Simon's House (Lk 7:36-50)
Jesus Instructs the Disciples (Mk 6:7-13)
The Sermon on the Mount (Mt 5–7)
Miracle of Cana (Jn 2:1-12)
"Who Do People Say I Am?" (Mt 16:13-17)
Curing of the Blind Man of Jericho (Lk 18:35-43)
The Miracle of the Loaves (Jn 6:1-13)
Jesus and Zacchaeus (Lk 19:1-10)
Raising of Lazarus (Jn 11:1-44)
The Rich Young Man (Mt 19:16-22)
Driving Out the Money Changers (Mk 11:15-17)
Washing the Apostles' Feet (Jn 13:1-20)
The Mount of Olives (Lk 22:39-46)
The Crucifixion (Lk 23:33-49)
The Disciples on the Way to Emmaus (Lk 24:13-35)

CONTEMPLATIVE PRAYER

Contemplative prayer is a special kind of prayer. Trappist Basil Pennington says that in this kind of prayer,

We go beyond thought and image, beyond the senses

and the rational mind, to that center of our being where God is working a wonderful work.[3]

Consider two people who are deeply in love. There are times when they can simply *be* with each other. They are silent together, enjoying each other's company whether sitting in the same room, taking a walk together, or enjoying a moonlit sky. This kind of comfortable being together usually comes only after the lovers have spent considerable time sharing and growing closer. Contemplative prayer can be compared to this special human experience.

One of my joys as a father has been to have my children crawl into my lap for me to read to them or tell them a story. Sometimes, though, we will just sit there together. My two youngest especially enjoy "cuddling Daddy." (I enjoy it too.) My arms encircle them and they sit quietly, snuggling up to their father. This is total love—a father for his children, the children for their daddy. For me, this is an excellent example of contemplative prayer. We allow the Father to encircle us with his love as we relax in the warmth of his life, compassion and concern for us. We need say nothing at all but simply "let go and let God" vitalize us with his presence, his goodness, his peace.

All Christians are called to contemplative prayer, to a close relationship of love with God. Contemplative prayer is sometimes called passive because we don't have to do anything except be ourselves and put ourselves in God's presence. Above all else, we should want to be united with God. We should desire to bask in the sunlight of God's love. We should want to rest in the arms of our loving *Abba* who has made us out of nothing and keeps up in his love.

Contemplative prayer is described in the biography of St. John Vianney. St. John knew of an old peasant who

---

[3] M. Basil Pennington, O.C.S.O., *Centering Prayer* (Garden City, New York: Image Books, 1982), p. 18.

used to spend hours and hours sitting motionless in the chapel, apparently doing nothing. When the saint asked him what he was doing all those hours, the old peasant replied, "I look at God, God looks at me, and we are happy."

Today contemplative prayer is growing in popularity because more people have discovered that this prayer gives us a profound sense of God's love. We can pray contemplatively alone, with a few others, or with a small group.

Centering Prayer

Centering prayer is an active prayer which can lead to the passive prayer of contemplation. It is a method to help us quiet down and be in the presence of the Lord.

Step 1:   Find a quiet place to pray. Relax by slowly inhaling and exhaling. Assume a comfortable position with your spine in a straight line. Close your eyes. Now move to the very center of your being. Become aware of God's presence. Express your faith in words such as these:

> Lord, I believe that you are present in me, at the very center of my existence, keeping me alive in your love. For my prayer period, I just want to be with you. Draw me close to you, Lord. Let me experience your presence and your love.

Step 2:   After a minute or so, select a special word that makes you think of God and his love. Recite this word over and over. The repetition will help keep distractions away. Choose a name, quality or title that carries deep meaning for you. Here are some examples:

Jesus	Father	Spirit
Lord	Abba	Love
Truth	Life	Way
Savior	Yahweh	Protector

After a short time you can stop reciting the word as you become aware of the Lord at the center of your being. If distractions come, and they often do, return to the word to refocus on God's loving presence.

Step 3:   At the end of your time of prayer, give thanks for God's presence to you. Tell Jesus of your love for him. Ask the Lord and his love to remain with you. Slowly and meditatively recite an Our Father.

Note: Ten to 20 minutes is a good time to spend on this centering prayer. Try it daily for two weeks and then reflect on your own reactions to this prayer.

The Jesus Prayer

Many people who pray the centering prayer grow into a deeper relationship with the Lord. They sense the power of his love. This love helps to transform them and make them more Christlike in their daily lives. They also become more joyful persons because they begin to experience God's love for them.

In recent years more and more Christians have also begun to pray the Jesus Prayer, an ancient Eastern Christian prayer. This prayer was developed first by the desert Fathers in response to the words of St. Paul:

> Always be joyful; pray constantly; and for all things give thanks; this is the will of God for you in Christ Jesus (1 Thes 5:17-18).

There are a number of variations of the Jesus Prayer, but the most common form is:

> Lord Jesus Christ, Son of God, have mercy on me, a sinner.

Many people recite this prayer as a centering prayer to prepare them for contemplation. But this simple prayer, which contains the essence of the gospel message, can be said anytime and anywhere. It can be said as a prelude to prayer, as a meditation or as a short prayer on any occasion when we feel moved to call on our God.

The Jesus Prayer is rooted in the gospels. When the blind Bartimaeus approached Jesus, he said, "Son of David, Jesus, have pity on me" (Mk 10:47). Also, recall from our scripture meditation how the ten men with the skin disease pleaded, "Jesus! Master! Take pity on us." Finally, look at the parable of the Pharisee and the tax collector (Lk 18:10-14). There the humble publican says, "God, be merciful to me, a sinner."

What is the Jesus Prayer saying? Let us look at it phrase by phrase.

Lord: By calling Jesus Lord, we are recognizing that he is the ruler of our lives.

Jesus: The name *Jesus* means "savior." In the God-made-man, eternal life has been won for us.

Christ: *Christ* means "anointed one," "Messiah." Jesus is the promised one who has come to establish God's kingdom of peace and justice both in our lives and in the world.

Son of God: Jesus is the unique offspring of God. Jesus is the Way to the Father, the Truth, and the Life.

have mercy: By asking for forgiveness and mercy, we are admitting that we need God's love, kindness, compassion and help.

on me: Here we ask God to remember us as individuals, to extend his loving mercy to us.

a sinner: Like the tax collector, we should approach God with humility, with a recognition of our need for healing.

Many people combine the words of the Jesus Prayer with their breathing. Try reciting it this way:

Inhale as you say: "Lord Jesus Christ"

Exhale as you say: "Son of God"

Inhale as you say: "have mercy on me"

Exhale as you say: "a sinner"

The words of the Jesus Prayer can become part of our lives, as close as the air we breathe. It is indeed a response to Paul's injunction to "Pray constantly."

A Prayer Reflection

The following journal exercise is a good way to meditate on scripture.

First, quiet down and find a good place to write. Ask the Holy Spirit to be with you and to guide your meditation.

Next, take a short passage from one of the gospels. Read it slowly, line by line, verse by verse. Observe. What do you see? feel? touch? hear? smell? Think. What is going on here? Listen. What is the Lord saying to you? Resolve to respond to any insight gained from the meditation.

Finally, write down your thoughts.

Here is a brief sample from Matthew 27:27-31, the mocking of Jesus:

> Lord, the day is very hot. The sun beats down on my head as I stand in Pilate's courtyard watching the people taunt you. The other apostles have fled away, but here I am, off in the distance, hiding behind a pillar. I don't want anyone to see me with you. They might turn on me, too.
>
> I see the scarlet robe they are putting on your bloody shoulders. How you must hurt! And the thorns of the mock crown they have made. I see you wince in pain and cry out. Oh, Lord, why are they

doing this to you? Now they are striking you with a reed. Some of the soldiers are laughing. They almost look drunk. I can't stand their loudness. It is stifling hot. I can even smell the blood.

Lord, how you suffer for me. They will shortly lead you off to Calvary where you will die for me. How much you love me! I would never think of mocking you and torturing you. But is that true? Didn't I put someone down yesterday? I didn't like the way she talked. I felt so superior. How immature of me. I now remember, Lord, that you said whatever I do to others, I do to you.

Forgive me, Lord, for not being faithful to you. I will try to extend a hand of friendship to the woman I hurt yesterday. Help me, Lord, to be more tolerant, to see you in everyone. Thank you, Lord, for your love. I am sorry for having hurt you.

A Scripture Reflection

"Two men went up to the Temple to pray, one a Pharisee, the other a tax collector. The Pharisee stood there and said this prayer to himself, 'I thank you, God, that I am not grasping, unjust, adulterous like everyone else, and particularly that I am not like this tax collector here. I fast twice a week; I pay tithes on all I get.' The tax collector stood some distance away, not daring even to raise his eyes to heaven; but he beat his breast and said, 'God, be merciful to me, a sinner.' This man, I tell you, went home again justified; the other did not. For everyone who raises himself up will be humbled, but anyone who humbles himself will be raised up" (Lk 18:10-14).

5
Praying With the Saints

As children and adolescents we undoubtedly had heroes, people we looked up to and admired because of who they were or what they had accomplished. As adults we may still respect and admire certain public figures. In addition, we might have personal heroes—mentors, friends, colleagues—who serve as models for us. We recognize that we are still in the process of becoming, and we look to others who seem to exemplify the qualities that we want for ourselves.

The Christian community also has its heroes, the saints. Saints were (and are) flesh-and-blood people like us. Saints laugh and cry, lose their tempers, have families and friends. They hold jobs. They love.

The quality that sets apart those the church has recognized as saints is their wholehearted commitment to become what God wants them to become. Saints have taken the following warning from the Book of Revelation to heart; they have made a decision:

> "I know about your activities: how you are neither cold nor hot. I wish you were one or the other, but since you are neither hot nor cold, but only lukewarm, I will spit you out of my mouth" (Rv 3:15-16).

We admire the saints because they have done something

that we know takes devotion, commitment and perseverance. They stand out as examples for us to admire and imitate.

No one became a saint without cultivating a friendship with the Lord. And prayer always played a central role in nourishing this relationship. By looking at the saints and what they can teach us about prayer, we can advance in our own journey with the Lord. We will look particularly at four saints: Mary, the Mother of God; St. Benedict; St. Francis of Assisi; and St. Therese of Lisieux.

MARY, THE MOTHER OF GOD

There is no doubt that the greatest of saints is Mary, the Mother of God. She provides an example to us, her spiritual children, of what it means to do the will of God. Mary exhibited many traits that make her a perfect model for Christian prayer.

Two essential qualities for a good prayer life are faith and humility. Faith, the virtue of trusting on the word of another, was at the heart of Mary's life. Not fully understanding why or how, Mary accepted in faith and trust the invitation to become God's mother:

"You see before you the Lord's servant, let it happen to me as you have said" (Lk 1:38).

Her humble and trusting response to God's desire to work through her serves as the kind of response we all owe our loving Creator.

Mary's trust in God's word helped bring forth the Word into human life. But Mary was also humble. She knew that all that was happening in and through her took place through God's power.

"For the almighty has done great things for me" (Lk 1:49).

Mary prayed often. We know that she rushed off to visit her cousin Elizabeth and sang joyfully with her of

God's great goodness. She went to the Temple frequently for the great feasts; we know she and Joseph presented Jesus at the time of her purification and that the family celebrated the Passover at the Temple when Jesus was 12. Undoubtedly Jesus learned his daily prayers from his parents, and through them he learned to revere the sacred Hebrew scriptures prayerfully studied in every pious Jewish home. After Jesus' ascension into heaven, Mary helped lead the early Christian community in prayer:

> With one heart all these joined constantly in prayer, together with some women, including Mary the mother of Jesus, and with his brothers (Acts 1:14).

Mary also shows us how to meditate and contemplate. In meditation we use our minds and imaginations to more deeply appreciate the great mysteries of God's love. By joining ourselves to the Lord in our meditation, we try to apply any insights we've gained to our daily life. Mary meditated throughout her life. For example, she meditated when the shepherds came to glorify God for the birth of the Savior:

> As for Mary, she treasured all these things and pondered them in her heart (Lk 2:19).

She must have prayerfully considered the words of the prophets Simeon and Anna, spoken when Jesus was presented in the Temple. And Mary undoubtedly carried with her for many years Jesus' words to her and Joseph after he was lost in the Temple for three days:

> He went down with them then and came to Nazareth and lived under their authority. His mother stored up all these things in her heart (Lk 2:51).

Mary is also an exemplary contemplative. In contemplation we seek to bask in the warmth of God's love; we delight in his presence. Few words are needed. Mary lived quietly in Nazareth with Jesus, God-become-man. This humble woman, without sin, recognized the Holy Spirit's presence in all of creation. Scripture records only a few of Mary's spoken words. Her prayer also was probably mostly wordless. She lived a life of love, joy and peace with a heart united to her Son and the Creator who blessed her among women.

Praying the Rosary

The most popular devotion to Mary—and an effective way to meditate—is the Rosary. The Rosary grew out of the practice of medieval monks who used to recite the 150 psalms. Since many monks did not know all of the psalms by heart or could not read, they substituted other prayers, usually 150 Our Fathers or Hail Marys. This devotion became popular with the laity. They used beads to help remember how many prayers they had recited.

St. Dominic is credited with popularizing the Rosary, but it has undergone some changes since his death in the 13th century. The complete Rosary consists of 15 decades. But it is divided into three distinct parts. Most rosary beads (*bead* comes from the Middle English word *bede* which meant "a prayer") are divided into five sets of ten Hail Marys with a single Glory Be and Our Father in between. These five decades are arranged in a circle. An additional part, which includes five additional beads and a crucifix, is used for introductory prayers.

It is customary to recite five decades of the Rosary at one time and to meditate on certain scenes or events—mysteries—from the lives of Jesus and Mary. The scenes are divided into three groups of five meditations. The first set of meditations includes the Joyful Mysteries, certain joyful events in the life of Jesus and Mary. The second set includes the Sorrowful Mysteries and are centered around Jesus' passion. The third set considers the Glorious Mysteries.

How do we pray the Rosary? We begin at the crucifix with a Sign of the Cross and then recite the Apostles'

Creed. We proceed to the next bead and recite the Our Father and then go to the next three beads (which symbolize either the Trinity or the theological virtues of faith, hope and love) praying three Hail Marys. We follow this with a Glory Be. After these preliminary prayers, we are ready to recite a decade of the Rosary.

Each decade of the Rosary begins by recalling a mystery or event from Jesus' or Mary's life. During the recitation of the prayers, aloud or silently, we will meditate on this event. Our meditation can take one of several forms. For example, we might place ourselves in the scene and imagine what great deeds have taken place on our behalf. Or we could reflect on one aspect of the scene; for example, the suffering of Jesus on the cross at the time of the crucifixion. Or we could take note of a virtue shown in the event and resolve to apply it to our lives; for example, Mary's generosity in undertaking a trip to visit her cousin Elizabeth.

After recalling the event and momentarily deciding how we will meditate on it, we say one Our Father and ten Hail Marys and one Glory Be, proceeding on to the next bead with each prayer. This completes one decade. All the other decades are recited in the same manner with a different event meditated on during each decade. At the end of the Rosary it is customary to recite the Hail, Holy Queen.

The recitation of the prayers during the Rosary, especially the Hail Marys, helps reduce distractions as we meditate on the mysteries. The Hail Mary developed over a long period of time. One of the most popular of all Christian prayers, the Hail Mary has scriptural roots and is composed of the following parts: the greeting of the Archangel Gabriel (Lk 1:28); Elizabeth's words to Mary (Lk 1:42); the sacred name of Jesus; and a formula of petition.

Mary is our mother who stands ready to intercede for us. Her faith and her love provide a model for us as we strive to follow her son. We can take great comfort in the following thought:

By her maternal charity, she cares for the brethren of her Son, who still journey on earth surrounded by dangers and difficulties, until they are led into their blessed home (*Dogmatic Constitution on the Church*, No. 62).

The Mysteries of the Rosary

Here is a review of the mysteries of the Rosary. In parentheses are a scriptural citation to the mystery and a word or two that will suggest an application to our own lives.

The Joyful Mysteries

1. The Annunciation (Lk 1:26-38; humility)
2. The Visitation of Mary to Elizabeth (Lk 1:41-56; love of neighbor)
3. The Birth of Jesus (Lk 2:1-7; God's love for us)
4. Presentation of Jesus in the Temple (Lk 2:22-23; obedience to God's law)
5. The Finding of Jesus in the Temple (Lk 2:41-50; faithfulness to one's calling)

The Sorrowful Mysteries

1. The Agony in the Garden (Mk 14:32-52; Jesus at prayer)
2. Scourging at the Pillar (Jn 19:1; suffering for others)
3. Crowning With Thorns (Mt 27:28-31; courage)
4. Carrying of the Cross (Jn 19:17; patience in suffering)
5. Crucifixion (Mt 27:32-38; supreme sacrifice of love)

The Glorious Mysteries

1. The Resurrection of Jesus (Jn 20:1; faith in new life)
2. The Ascension of Jesus Into Heaven (Mt 16:19; hope in eternal life)
3. The Descent of the Holy Spirit (Acts 2:4; the giving of gifts: wisdom, understanding, zeal, love, fortitude, etc.)
4. The Assumption of Mary Into Heaven (Rv 12:1-6; eternal happiness for which all are destined)

5. The Coronation of Mary as Queen of Heaven (Rv 12:1; devotion to Mary and her everlasting care for us)

SAINT BENEDICT

St. Benedict founded the famous monastery of Monte Cassino around the year 520. From this community, Benedict wrote a famous *Rule* for his monks that was to become the monastic rule for the Western church. It was a balanced, practical rule that became the most influential guide to the spiritual life in medieval history.

What can Benedict's ancient Rule teach us about prayer? St. Benedict attempted to find a balance among three things: public prayer at set times throughout the day (called the "work of God"), the constant reading and meditation on the Bible (called "divine reading"), and manual work for the physical and economic support of the whole monastery.

Benedict's motto was *ora et labora*, "pray and work." By doing this faithfully, those who live a monastic life can grow in friendship before God. Monastic life also provides an example to others of how Christians might live in peace and harmony. Those who choose to live this way are also saying to the world, *Look, we are dedicated to the coming of God's kingdom without being attached to the passing things of this world.* Their witness forces those of us who choose to live in the world to question what we are doing and helps us look more seriously at our own level of commitment to God.

We can learn much from Benedict's instructions on how to do "divine reading," a very popular form of prayer. His directions are simple, comprising three steps:

Lectio (or sacred reading)

Meditatio (or meditation)

Oratio (or prayer)

Step 1—Reading

Select a reading from scripture (perhaps from Psalms or the New Testament), a famous prayer, an important book in spirituality such as Thomas à Kempis' *The Imitation of Christ* or some other devotional book. Quiet yourself in God's presence.

Begin reading and continue until a passage, a line, a phrase strikes you. At this point, stop and begin your meditation.

For our example, let's take a reading from St. Paul's letter to the Philippians beginning with chapter 2:

> So if in Christ there is anything that will move you, any incentive in love, any fellowship in the Spirit, any warmth or sympathy—I appeal to you, make my joy complete by being of a single mind, one in love, one in heart and one in mind. Nothing is to be done out of jealousy or vanity; instead, out of humility of mind everyone should give preference to others, everyone pursuing not selfish interests but those of others (Phil 2:1-4).

Let's say that the last sentence strikes you. Stop here and begin your meditation.

Step 2—Meditation

In this stage, you pause, let the meaning of the verse or words sink into your mind and heart. Mentally repeat the words over and over again. Let them become part of you: *Everyone should give preference to others*. Relish the words. Appreciate what they are saying. Let the meaning sink in. After spending some time pondering the words, turn to the prayer.

Step 3—Prayer

Speak to God about the verse or simply sit in God's

presence and let the Lord speak to you. You might pray something like this:

> Do you mean I should do this all the time, Lord? It is so hard sometimes for me to give preference to others. You know how selfish I can be. And some of these others I meet every day are very unloving toward me. But perhaps they would change if I treated them better. I'm reminded of how you silently endured the taunts of your tormentors. Help me treat others in a good way, Lord. I know I can't do it alone. I need your help.

When you find that you have exhausted your prayer or you become distracted, return to the passage again and begin to read until you come to another phrase that seems to be speaking directly to you. Then begin the process over again.

Some other passages that lend themselves to this type of prayer are other readings from Paul's letters. These are especially good for beginners in this type of prayer:

Spiritual gifts (1 Cor 12:4-31)

Overcome evil with good (Rom 12:9-21)

Love is patient and kind (Col 3:12-17)

Live by the Spirit of God (Gal 5:16-26)

SAINT FRANCIS OF ASSISI

Next to Mary, St. Francis of Assisi (c. 1181-1226) is probably the most popular Christian saint. His joyous, simple and outgoing nature, which was dedicated to the spread of God's kingdom, gained him the nickname "Troubadour for Christ." His literal interpretation of Mark 10:21—"Go and sell what you own and give the money to the poor"—earned him the additional sobriquet "The Little Poor Man."

Before his conversion Francis was a rich young man who enjoyed indulging in the pleasure of a carefree life and in the excitement of petty wars. After a lengthy imprisonment, a serious illness and a powerful religious vision, his life changed dramatically. He went to Rome on pilgrimage in 1206 and then devoted himself to a life of poverty, caring for the sick and the poor.

His choice was not popular with his family; his father disinherited him. But Francis did not turn away from his commitment. After repairing some ruined churches, he attracted numerous followers and founded a religious community which was approved by the pope. Francis and his friars dedicated themselves to a life of service to the poor and to spreading the good news of God's love.

What gave life to Francis' vision was a single-hearted commitment to our Lord Jesus. He sensed God's love everywhere. And he continuously lived a prayerful response to that love.

Francis has much to teach us about prayer. He had a great devotion to the infant Jesus, building a crib at Christmas in the year 1223. The Christmas crib became a custom that is still honored today. He often meditated on the passion and suffering of Christ. In 1224 he received the stigmata, which remained with him to the end of his life.

Francis never ceased teaching that God is a loving Father, and that we should not be afraid to approach him in simple, childlike prayer. Francis also taught the importance of praising and thanking God. He composed many prayers. One of the most famous attributed to him is the "Canticle of Brother Sun" (see Appendix, page 134). This prayer typifies Francis' mystical vision. Francis believed that God can be found in all of creation: in sunrises and sunsets, in the smile on an infant's face, in a sparrow flying across a field, in a gentle, babbling brook, in grass growing, in leaves falling. His response, and the response he teaches all of us to make, is to praise and thank God for all that he has made and all he has given us.

Another prayer usually attributed to St. Francis is the familiar "Prayer for Peace."

Lord, make me an instrument of your peace,
where there is hatred, let me sow love;
where there is injury, pardon;
where there is doubt, faith;
where there is despair, hope;
where there is darkness, light;
where there is sadness, joy.

O Divine Master, grant that I may seek
  not so much
to be consoled as to console,
to be understood, as to understand,
to be loved, as to love.

For it is in giving that we receive,
it is in pardoning that we are pardoned,
and it is in dying that we are born to eternal life.

The meditation on this prayer could become an excellent "action prayer." As you contemplate each phrase, think of examples of hatred, injury, doubt, despair, darkness and sadness in the following situations:

- in the world at large
- in your country
- in your community
- where you work
- in your home

Ask the Lord to help you see how you can bring pardon, faith, hope, light, joy and consolation to at least one of these situations.

ST. THERESE OF LISIEUX

The facts of St. Therese's life are simple enough. She was born in 1873 in France, the youngest of nine children of Louis Martin, a watchmaker, and his wife, Zelie. Her mother died when Therese was five; she was raised by her older sisters and an aunt.

Two of Therese's sisters became Carmelite nuns, and Therese followed in their footsteps at the unprecedented age of 15. She took the name Therese of the Child Jesus. While in the convent she contracted tuberculosis and died at the age of 24. At the insistence of two mother superiors (one her sister Pauline), Therese wrote her life's story entitled *The Story of a Soul*. It was completed shortly before her death. This remarkable autobiography has become one of the most widely read classics of the spiritual life.

What can we learn from a young nun who lived 100 years ago? Why does she remain one of the most popular saints of our century? What was it about her that inspired both French generals and ordinary soldiers during World War I to carry a copy of her life with them and look to her as a symbol of bravery?

Therese was what most of us would like to be: a person totally dedicated to the love of Jesus Christ. Therese also shows us that we don't have to be among the famous people of the world to be a saint. She called her journey to God the "Little Way." With God's help, we can all follow the Little Way; it is the way of love, of doing the most ordinary things in an extraordinary way, or accepting whatever God sends to us.

Therese underwent the kind of trials that each of us experiences. For example, she went out of her way to help a tired, complaining old nun. Nothing Therese did made the nun happy, but she continued to help her, accepting abuse and not talking back.

In her autobiography Therese also tells of her fierce temper and her impatience. She continually fought against these. When one nun made a habit of splashing her in the face at the wash pool, Therese kept silent, offering this little humiliation to the Lord. When another nun made an annoying clacking noise in chapel, Therese wanted to scream "Enough!" Instead, she offered her annoyance as a prayer to Jesus and found a certain kind of peace in doing so.

We can all identify with Therese. It is hard to accept daily the little crosses that come into our lives. It is difficult to listen to people who bore us. It takes courage to hold our tongues when our patience is stretched to the breaking point. It requires tremendous strength to go out of our way to help someone who doesn't like us or whom we find unattractive. And nothing is harder than suffering and not letting others know about it.

Therese does not teach a complicated method of praying. She herself admitted to falling asleep during her prayers. But she said that God loved her just the same, just as parents love their children as much when they are asleep as when they are awake. Here is what Therese says about prayer. We can all learn from her simple, yet profound message.

> I behave like children who cannot read: I tell God very simply what I want and He always understands. For me, prayer is an upward leap of the heart, an untroubled glance toward heaven, a cry of gratitude and love which I utter from the depths of sorrow as well as from the heights of joy.[1]

Therese's basic message is very simple. We should live every day as though it were our last. We should take everything that comes to us as a final opportunity to respond to the Lord Jesus before meeting him at the end of the day. We should do the most ordinary of things in an extraordinary way because this may be our last opportunity to do them. True love does not hold back; it does not hedge. It gives itself totally. In "The Eternal Today" Therese teaches:

---

[1] *The Autobiography of St. Therese of Lisieux: The Journal of a Soul,* trans. and Introduction by John Beevers (Garden City, New York: Image Books, 1957), p. 136.

My life is an instant,
An hour which passes by;
My life is a moment
Which I have no power to stay.
You know, O my God,
That to love you here on earth—
I have only today.[2]

St. Therese's favorite image of Jesus came from the gospel account of the storm at sea (Mk 4:35-41). At times she went through some rough waters, but she always trusted that Jesus was present, even if he was asleep in the boat.

Read and meditate on Mark 4:35-41. Think about a time when the going was rough and you felt abandoned. How did the Lord help you?

A Prayer Reflection

Imagine that you have only today left before you meet the Lord. Respond to the following questions in your journal:

1. Briefly describe a situation at home or at work that has been "getting under your skin" of late. Write the initials of the person who seems to be causing most of the problems in the situation you have described. Consider what you might do to accept this cross more pleasantly.

2. If you were to die at midnight tonight, whom would you most want to see before you die? What would you say to the person?

3. List the three most important gifts that God has given you. If you were to meet the Lord tonight, to whom would you will your gifts? How has each of these gifts helped you

---

[2] Cited by Gloria Hutchinson in *Six Ways to Pray from Six Great Saints* (Cincinnati: St. Anthony Messenger Press, 1982), p. 101.

draw closer to God? Why did you choose to leave certain gifts to certain people in your imaginary will?

A Scripture Reflection

"My soul proclaims the greatness of the Lord
and my spirit *rejoices in God my Savior;*
because *he has looked upon the humiliation of his servant.*
Yes, from now onwards all generations will call me blessed,
for the Almighty has done great things for me.
Holy is his name,
and *his faithful love extends age after age to those who fear him*" (Lk 1:46-50).

6
Spiritual Classics

In the previous chapter we turned to four great Christian saints for their guidance in prayer. In the present chapter we will continue to look for advice and encouragement by highlighting some of the classic writings on prayer.

In deciding what to include in this discussion I was concerned that the works be readable and easy to understand, appropriate for the novice in prayer as well as the more mature pray-er. The works of St. John of the Cross and St. Teresa of Avila rank with the greatest of spiritual writing. Some commentators suggest that the writings of these two spiritual masters are the norm against which all other classics should be measured. But, in my judgment, they are not easy going, so I decided not to discuss them here. I only include works that I believe a beginner in prayer can pick up, read and understand without the help of a commentator.

The Cloud of Unknowing

A rediscovered and increasingly popular spiritual work is a book originally written in Middle English by an unknown author. Little is known about the origins of *The Cloud of Unknowing* and its companion treatise, *The Book of Privy Counselling,* other than that they were composed sometime in the late 14th century and are steeped in the medieval church and its spirituality. Their objective is to guide the reader in contemplation.

Contemplation seeks union with God by helping the pray-er to go beyond any thoughts, concepts and images of God in order simply to rest in the Lord's presence. *The Cloud of Unknowing* counsels this type of prayer because God is beyond all thoughts and concepts and beyond all images. God is love and he can only be grasped in love. Contemplation of God as he is in himself is a gift of God himself; to respond to this grace is to love.

> Thought cannot comprehend God. And so, I prefer to abandon all I can know, choosing rather to love him whom I cannot know. Though we cannot know him we can love him. By love he may be touched and embraced, never by thought.[1]

The author of *The Cloud* instructs the reader simply to focus on God as God is, a God whom we cannot conceptualize or imagine. Our minds should be kept in complete darkness, in a *cloud of unknowing.* To contemplate, though, also requires that you

> concern yourself with no creature whether material or spiritual nor with their situation and doings whether good or ill. To put it briefly, during this work you must abandon them all beneath the *cloud of forgetting* (p. 53).

The objective in contemplative prayer is to love God as he is, to forget all thoughts, to leave behind all preconceptions, to allow the being of the hidden God to touch our being.

> For in real charity one loves God for himself alone above every created thing and he loves his fellow man

---

[1] *The Cloud of Unknowing and the Book of Privy Counselling,* ed. with Introduction by William Johnston (Garden City, New York: Doubleday, Image Books, 1973), p. 54.

because it is God's law. In the contemplative work God is loved above every creature purely and simply for his sake. Indeed the very heart of this work is nothing else but a naked intent toward God for his own sake (p. 80).

Contemplation, then, is to enter into a loving union with God. This union is the summit of Christian life. *The Cloud of Unknowing* teaches us that contemplation is the greatest work we can do because through it we are loving God above everything and everyone. Its benefits are many; for example, because we allow Love to touch us, we are enabled to love others more ardently. In addition, contact with Love helps heal us of our spiritual ills. Furthermore, God will provide for our needs:

> You can be certain of this: he will provide one of two things for his friends. Either they will receive an abundance of all they need or he will give them the physical stamina and a patient heart to endure want. What difference does it make which he does? (p. 79).

This promise can be a great encouragement to us as we develop our prayer life.

The Cloud of Unknowing deals with lofty thoughts; at the same time, it is very practical. In it we find a simple method of prayer that anyone who strives for union with God can find very helpful.

> So whenever you feel drawn by grace to the contemplative work and are determined to do it, simply raise your heart to God with a gentle stirring of love. Think only of God, the God who created you, redeemed you, and guided you to this work. . . . Gather all your desire into one simple word that the mind can easily retain, choose a short word rather than a long one. A one-syllable word such as "God" or "love" is best. But choose one that is meaningful to you. Then fix it in your mind so that it will remain there come what may. This word will be your defense in conflict and in peace (p. 56).

The Imitation of Christ

Without a doubt, *The Imitation of Christ* is one of the greatest of all spiritual classics. With the exception of the Bible itself, no other devotional book or spiritual classic has been read as widely. It has had a profound influence on subsequent spiritual masters—notably St. Ignatius Loyola—and has provided rich spiritual strength for countless Christians down through the centuries. Its spiritual wisdom still speaks clearly to our own generation.

Authorship of *The Imitation of Christ* is attributed to Thomas à Kempis (1379/80-1471). He was a German who lived at a time of turmoil in church-state relations, of conflict in church politics (at one time three men claimed to be pope), and of considerable laxity in living out the Christian message (for example, dissension in monasteries and convents). He joined a small community founded by Gerard Groote which went by the name "The Brothers of the Common Life." They desired to live a deeper spirituality to help counteract the lukewarm religious life of their day; they also wished to promote sound learning.

Thomas was ordained at the age of 33 and subsequently held several positions of authority in his religious community. During the last 20 years or so of his life, though, he led the quiet life of a counselor, student, copyist and writer, producing a remarkable quantity of work.

His most highly regarded work is *The Imitation of Christ* which was completed around 1427. It reflects the spirituality of his religious community, one that went by the name of "modern devotion." *Devotio moderna* appealed to a simple piety of the heart, in contrast with the excessive intellectual mysticism in vogue at the time. The most famous passage from *The Imitation of Christ* underscores the major approach taken throughout:

> I would rather feel compunction [remorse] of heart for my sins than merely know the definition of compunction. If you know all the books of the Bible

merely by rote and all the sayings of the philosophers by heart, what will it profit you without grace and charity? All that is in the world is vanity except to love God and to serve Him only. This is the most noble and the most excellent wisdom that can be in any creature: by despising the world to draw daily nearer and nearer to the kingdom of heaven.[2]

To the modern reader this passage might seem anti-intellectual and negative, especially toward the world. There is some truth in this charge, but we should remember that *The Imitation of Christ* was written by a monk for monks who were attempting to withdraw from their troubled world in order to follow Christ more closely.

We live in an age which usually sees the external world in a more positive light than our ancestors in the faith did. But our world is also a dangerous place; there are all kinds of temptations that pull us away from following Christ. The four sections of *The Imitation of Christ*—admonitions useful for the spiritual life, admonitions leading to the inner life, how Christ speaks to the Christian, and a discussion of the Eucharist—have much wisdom for the Christian who wishes to follow Jesus more closely. *The Imitation of Christ* also contains many beautiful prayers and is loaded with "quotable quotes" that are worthy of our personal reflection and meditation. For example,

How great a vanity it also is to desire a long life and to care little for a good life (p. 32).

On the day of judgment we will not be asked what we have read, but what we have done; not how well we have discoursed, but how religiously we have lived (p. 35).

Fire proves gold, and temptation proves the righteous man (p. 45).

---

[2] Thomas à Kempis, The *Imitation of Christ,* ed. with Introduction by Harold C. Gardiner, S.J. (Garden City, New York: Doubleday, Image Books, 1955), p. 32.

Today a man; tomorrow none. When you are out of sight you are soon out of mind, and soon will be forgotten. Oh, the great dullness and hardness of man's heart, which thinks only about present things and gives little care to the life to come. If you acted well, you should so behave in every deed and every thought as though you were about to die this very instant (p. 63).

Simplicity is in the intention; purity is in the love (p. 80).

A wise lover does not so much consider the gift of his lover as he does the love of the giver (p. 112).

Do not let your peace depend on the hearts of men; whatever they say about you, good or bad, you are not because of it another man, for as you are, you are (p. 147).

The Spiritual Exercises

Ranking high on the list of great spiritual classics is the *Spiritual Exercises* of St. Ignatius of Loyola (1491-1556). The details of Ignatius' life are well known. A Basque nobleman, Ignatius was wounded in the right leg while in military service; during his lengthy recovery he read a life of Christ and biographies of the saints. This revolutionized his life; from then on, he was determined to become "a soldier for Christ."

After his recovery Ignatius made a pilgrimage to Monserrat and then spent the year 1522-1523 on retreat at Manresa. It was here that the bulk of his *Spiritual Exercises* (published later in 1548) was probably written. From 1524-1535 Ignatius studied at various universities. In 1534 he founded the Society of Jesus with five fellow students at the University of Paris. The Society was formally approved in 1540 and became a driving force in the church of his day: fighting heresy at the time of the Reformation; engaging in massive missionary efforts; and working for church reform, especially through education and a greater devotion to the sacramental life. Today the Jesuits are the largest religious community of men in the Catholic church.

The *Spiritual Exercises* is a collection of admonitions, instructions, meditations, examinations of conscience and other religious devotions designed to bring true spiritual freedom, that is, a freedom from anything that might keep a person from serving God wholeheartedly.

The foundation of the *Spiritual Exercises* is the statement that "God freely created us so that we might know, love, and serve him in this life and be happy with him forever."[3] All things God has created are gifts whose purpose is to get us to know him better, love him more deeply and serve him more faithfully. Thus, we should use God's gifts in such a way that they help us achieve our goal of love, service and union with God. The Exercises are designed to help us let go of any created thing which would hinder the purpose for which we are made. They are geared to free us to devote ourselves to God's greater honor and glory.

The *Spiritual Exercises* is not light reading in the sense of a devotional book on popular piety. Rather, it is written more for a retreat director who is guiding a retreatant. The Exercises are meant to be lived rather than merely read. Ignatius originally intended that they be made over a 30-day period, but various adaptations include three-day and eight-day retreats as well as a "life-in-the-world" retreat which can take months for those who can devote only an hour or so daily to prayer. Those who wish to make an Ignatian retreat at home will profit greatly from using *A Vacation With the Lord* by Thomas H. Green, S.J. (see bibliography) along with the *Spiritual Exercises*.

The *Spiritual Exercises* is divided into four sections, called "weeks," although there is no set number of days in

---

[3] David L. Fleming, S.J., *Modern Spiritual Exercises: A Contemporary Reading of "The Spiritual Exercises of St. Ignatius"* (Garden City, New York: Doubleday, Image Books, 1978), p. 25.

each section. The First Week is devoted to a systematic consideration of sin and its consequences. The Second Week focuses on the life of Jesus, from his conception through his public ministry. The Third Week centers on Jesus' passion and death while the Fourth looks to the risen and glorified Christ.

The *Spiritual Exercises* teaches various methods of prayer; for example, it is an excellent resource on how to meditate, especially with scripture and on the life of Christ. St. Ignatius teaches us to put ourselves in God's presence, vividly imagine the subject of our meditation, reflect on the message the subject speaks to our heart and fervently ask that the grace of our prayer become part of our life.

Another key value of the *Spiritual Exercises* is to help us discern God's will for us. St. Ignatius strongly believed that God is vitally active in the world, and that he has a special call to service for all his children. The Exercises are designed to help us discover the gentle nudges of God's call and to unmask the subtle deceits of the evil spirits which tempt us to be spiritually flabby or unfaithful to the call to serve. The Exercises are especially recommended for someone who has a major life decision to make.

A wonderful Ignatian meditation comes from the Fourth Week, "Contemplation on the Love of God." It is reproduced at the end of the chapter and will serve as our concluding prayer reflection.

Introduction to the Devout Life

An evergreen among the spiritual classics is St. Francis de Sales' *Introduction to the Devout Life*. Francis de Sales (1567-1622) was a Frenchman who became bishop of the triple see of Geneva-Lausanne-Annecy, a territory in the heart of Protestant country at the time of the Reformation. He was a gentle spirit, a bishop who took seriously his responsibility of shepherding souls. He heard confessions, preached sermons, gave personal instructions in the faith, wrote letters, and became a prolific author of pamphlets and books which both explained and defended the Catholic faith. For his brilliant insights as a teacher, he is honored as a Doctor of the Church; because of his originality, clarity and style as an author, he is recognized as the patron saint of journalists and the Catholic press.

St. Francis de Sales had a generous heart and people were attracted to him. He was the spiritual director of St. Jane Frances de Chantal, and with her founded the Order of the Visitation. Francis de Sales' motto was *Vivat Jesus,* "Jesus lives." He was firmly convinced that a life of holiness, what he calls the "devout life," is open to all people including the lay person living in the world. *Introduction to the Devout Life* had its origins in letters Francis wrote to his friends and sister, encouraging them to follow the path to holiness. This path is found by hating sin, by freeing oneself from the things of the world, and by loving God, Francis encourages his readers to pray constantly to achieve these goals.

Introduction to the Devout Life is divided into five sections. The purpose of Part One is to help bring about a total turning away from sin, not only mortal sin which separates us from God, but also from slight offenses and from all our evil inclinations. St. Francis helps us accomplish this goal by carefully guiding us through ten meditations whose purpose is to purge us from any attachment to sin. These meditations—on themes like creation, God's gifts, death, judgment, hell and paradise—are timeless; they can enflame the heart of even the most sophisticated modern reader.

Part Two of the *Introduction to the Devout Life* contains instructions on effective ways to receive the sacraments, especially the Eucharist and reconciliation, and teachings about prayer. Francis encourages the practice of mental prayer, the prayer of the heart, especially advising reflection on the life and passion of Jesus. He teaches a structured method of meditation which is very easy to follow. It consists of the following steps:

1. *Preparation.*   Always put yourself in God's presence before beginning to pray. Ask for his help during your prayer session. And, if it is appropriate to do so, vividly imagine the mystery on which you are going to meditate. Francis offers several effective ways that help put the pray-er in God's presence:

    - Realize that God is "in all things and all places."
    - Recall that God is especially present in your heart, "in the very center of your spirit."
    - Imagine Jesus gazing at you from heaven while you are at prayer.
    - Picture Jesus next to you, as you might imagine a friend next to you.

2. *Consideration.*   After preparing for prayer, select a point or two to mull over, reflecting on the spiritual meaning. If you are meditating on the Annunciation, for example, you might ponder how Mary was ready to hear the angel because she made time to pray. Her life must have been one of openness and expectation. St. Francis advises us to remain with a topic if we derive some benefit from it, but to calmly move on to another if we can't extract "any honey out of it."

3. *Affections and Resolutions.*   Our considerations should produce feelings of love for God, compassion, awe, joy and the like. These feelings should lead us to make resolutions to improve our life. St. Francis gives an example:

    The first word our Lord spoke on the cross will undoubtedly excite in your soul a holy longing to imitate him, namely, a desire to pardon your enemies and to love them. . . . From now on I will not be offended by the disagreeable words a man or woman . . . says to me.[4]

4. *Conclusion and Spiritual Bouquet.*   St. Francis advises us to conclude our period of prayer by thanking God for what he has given us during our time of prayer, by offering up our resolutions in union with the Lord and by petitioning him to help us keep our resolutions. He encourages us to conclude by praying for the church, its ministers, our relatives and friends and all who need our prayers, after which we should pray the Our Father and Hail Mary.

Finally, St. Francis tells us to choose a point or two from our meditation to savor during the day. He encourages us to come back to these points from time to time to remember the sweetness of our time at prayer.

Part Three of the *Introduction to the Devout Life* provides many practical hints on how to live a virtuous life. St. Francis takes up topics like humility, obedience and chastity. He gives advice on how to avoid vices like rash judgment and slander. He offers spiritual counsel for widows, virgins and those who are married. In addition, he has a marvelous, and remarkably timely, section on the nature of true friendship.

Part Four offers some wise words on how to fight the various temptations that confront the Christian who has entrusted his or her life to the Lord. In the fifth part of the *Introduction to the Devout Life*, St. Francis calls for an annual renewal of our initial resolutions to live the devout life and a personal spiritual checkup which also focuses on

---

[4] St. Francis de Sales, *Introduction to the Devout Life,* trans. and ed. by John K. Ryan (Garden City, New York: Doubleday, Image Books, 1966), p. 89.

our relations with God and neighbor. He concludes by encouraging us to persevere in our good works.

St. Francis is a good writer. His spiritual insights and advice for living a prayerful life can help the novice as well as the more seasoned pray-er. He uses many pithy, down-to-earth similes and metaphors, ones that display a man in touch with both the natural universe and the human psyche. Undoubtedly, many of his maxims were written with a twinkle in his eye. Perhaps the following examples will tempt you to seek out St. Francis de Sales and his *Introduction to the Devout Life*.

On humility:

Just as honor is an excellent thing, when given to us freely, so also it becomes base when demanded, sought after, and asked for. A peacock spreads his tail in self-admiration and by the very act of raising up his beautiful feathers he ruffles all the others and displays his own ugliness. Flowers that are beautiful as they grow in the earth wither and fade when plucked (p. 133).

Spiritual poverty:

There is a difference between having poison and being poisoned. Pharmacists keep almost every kind of poison in stock for use on various occasions, yet they are not themselves poisoned because they merely have it in their shops and not in their bodies. So also you can possess riches without being poisoned by them if you merely keep them in your home and purse and not in your heart (p. 162).

On slander:

Whenever I speak of my neighbor, the tongue in my mouth is like a scalpel in the hand of a surgeon who wishes to cut between the nerves and the tendons. The stroke I give must be neither more nor less than the truth (p. 205).

The Practice of the Presence of God

The Practice of the Presence of God is the product of the spiritual life of Brother Lawrence of the Resurrection (c. 1606-1691). Born in the region of Lorraine, France, his name was Nicholas Herman. At the age of 18 he was a soldier in the Thirty Years War. The experiences of war, including his own wounding and capture, so deeply affected him that he decided to commit his life totally to Christ. In 1642 in a Carmelite community in Paris he professed vows as a simple lay brother in charge of the kitchen. He cheerfully performed menial tasks in this job and later in the shoe-repair shop.

Brother Lawrence acquired a reputation for holiness that touched the lives of people beyond the monastery walls. After a slow advance in the spiritual life, Brother Lawrence discovered and began to practice a simple but profound form of prayer. It is known as "the practice of the presence of God," that is, a sense in all activities, at all times of the day, and in all places, of God's abiding presence.

Brother Lawrence knew that the reason to pray is to achieve union with God. He felt the way to achieve this is through practicing the presence of God which he defines this way:

> The presence of God is the applying of our spirit to God, or a realization of the presence of God, which can be brought about either by the imagination or understanding.[5]

The method is quite simple. When we awake each morning, we should recall God's presence all around us. We should devote ourselves entirely to God, offering in simple faith whatever might be sent to us during the course

---

[5] Brother Lawrence of the Resurrection, *The Practice of the Presence of God,* trans. with an Introduction by John J. Delaney, Foreword by Henri J. M. Nouwen (Garden City, New York: Doubleday, Image Books, 1977), p. 107.

of the day. We should continually talk to God as we go about our activities, always sensing that God is right there with us, especially in the people who come into our lives. Brother Lawrence teaches that we can and should talk with God all the time, even while doing our routine tasks, and not only during formal prayer times. At the end of our day, we examine our consciences to see how well we have succeeded at our prayer. If we find that we have failed somewhat, we should cheerfully renew our purpose and begin again to practice the presence of God as if we had never stopped doing so.

The teachings of Brother Lawrence were collected together after his death by the Abbe de Beaufort and published in a short work which includes a recollection of his conversations, several of his letters and some spiritual maxims. The book is very easy to read and teaches a remarkable spiritual practice that can help us grow in holiness.

The Way of a Pilgrim

St. Paul teaches us to "always be joyful; *pray constantly*; for all things give thanks; this is the will of God for you in Christ Jesus" (1 Thes 5:17). Brother Lawrence of the Resurrection teaches us one way to do this, but so does an anonymous 19th-century Russian author in a fascinating work entitled *The Way of a Pilgrim*.

This delightful spiritual classic can be read on a number of levels. It can be read simply as an adventure story of a wandering pilgrim in search of knowledge; on a deeper level it can be read as a type for the spiritual quest of all true Christians, a quest which involves achieving union with God. *The Good Way of a Pilgrim* is a compendium of the spiritual wisdom of great Orthodox Christian theologians. Drawing on the teachings of the desert Fathers and those holy Fathers compiled in the *Philokalia,* our Pilgrim teaches us the ejaculatory prayer known as the Jesus Prayer (see page 63).

The Jesus Prayer is also known as the prayer of the heart. It contains within it the summary of the gospel. When we begin to pray the Jesus Prayer, we think out and verbalize the prayer: "Lord Jesus Christ, have mercy on me, a sinner." Thus the prayer is in the intellect and on the lips. But as we unceasingly persevere in the prayer, we find the place in the heart where the prayer becomes not a conscious effort of our intellects but a spontaneous uplifting of our whole being. This prayer of the heart is not achieved by our efforts but by the work of God's spirit.

The Way of a Pilgrim teaches that there are many consolations that can result from the prayer of the heart, spiritual fruits that can be experienced in the spirit, emotions and revelations:

> In the spirit one can experience the sweetness of the love of God, inner peace, purity of thought, awareness of God's presence, and ecstasy. In the emotions a pleasant warmth of the heart, a feeling of delight throughout one's being, joyful bubbling in the heart, lightness and courage, joy of life, and indifference to sickness and sorrow. And in revelation one receives the enlightenment of the mind, understanding of Holy Scripture, knowledge of speech of all creatures, renunciation of vanities, awareness of the sweetness of interior life, and confidence in the nearness of God and His love for us.[6]

These promised benefits might well prompt us to learn the Jesus Prayer and begin to make it part of our prayer life. At the least, the Pilgrim assures us that "When I began to pray with the heart, everything around me became transformed and I saw it in a new and delightful way" (p. 34). Practicing the presence of God or praying the prayer of the heart has greatly helped many people see God working in all things and meeting us in all people.

---

[6] *The Way of a Pilgrim and The Pilgrim Continues His Way,* trans. by Helen Bacovin, Foreword by Walter J. Ciszek, S.J. (Garden City, New York: Doubleday, Image Books, 1978), p. 41.

Thomas Merton

If we were to select the most significant writers on spirituality and prayer in the 20th century, we would have to include the name of Thomas Merton. His towering influence is greatly felt today, two decades after his bizarre, accidental death by electrocution while at a spiritual conference in Bangkok, Thailand, in 1968.

Thomas Merton was born in France in 1915. After a colorful youth and a stormy academic career, Merton converted to Catholicism, taught for a year at a Franciscan university and in 1941 entered the Trappist monastery of Gethsemani in Kentucky where he became known as Father Louis. Here he lived the life of a monk. At the same time, he wrote prolifically, over 60 books and hundreds of articles. His published works and his enormous correspondence touched the minds and hearts of everyone who read them.

In many ways, Merton was a Renaissance man. He was interested in the world of his day: literature, scientific developments, politics, people's spiritual quests. But the dominant theme in all of his writings is prayer. Prayer, for Merton, is the "consciousness of one's union with God," and "an awareness of one's inner self." He saw these two themes as identical. When I find my true self, I find myself-united-to God. When I pray, I am discovering this consciously.

To discover who we are as united to God, Merton tells us, we need interior solitude. To quiet down and get in touch with the inner life is essential for the spiritual life, for prayer. The purpose of prayer is not to escape life but to engage it to the full.

> The more I become identified with God [in prayer], the more will I be identified with all the others who

are identified with Him. His Love will live in all of us.
His Spirit will be our One Life.[7]

Merton's writings provide an embarrassment of riches
for the person who wishes to learn from a 20th-century
master who is truly in touch with our world and with our
modern spiritual odyssey. Merton's autobiography, *The
Seven Storey Mountain*, is reminiscent of St. Augustine's
Confessions. Some consider his short work *Contemplative
Prayer* his most polished gem on the topic of prayer. A collection like *A Thomas Merton Reader*[8] exposes the reader
to the scope of Merton's literary concerns. I would like to
recommend, though, his *New Seeds of Contemplation*.
Merton's reflections in this work have been compared with
those of Thoreau. They provide a wonderful sample of
Merton's thought; the chapters on contemplation, mental
prayer and distraction are most helpful.

The following passage hints at the simple profundity
of Merton:

> No matter how distracted you may be, try by peace-
> ful, even perhaps inarticulate, efforts to center your
> heart upon God, Who is present to you in spite of all
> that may be going through your mind. His presence
> does not depend on your thoughts of Him. He is un-
> failingly there; if He were not, you could not even ex-
> ist. The memory of His unfailing presence is the surest
> anchor for our minds and hearts in the storm of dis-
> traction and temptation by which we must be purified
> (*New Seeds of Contemplation*, p. 224).

The classics of the spiritual life need not frighten away
the beginner in prayer. All the works discussed in this
chapter can greatly enrich everyone's spiritual journey.

---

[7] Thomas Merton, *New Seeds of Contemplation* (New York: New Directions Books, 1961), p. 65.

[8] *A Thomas Merton Reader,* rev. ed., ed. by Thomas P. McDonnell (Garden City, New York: Doubleday, Image Books, 1974).

A Prayer Reflection

St. Ignatius Loyola teaches us the joy and freedom of the Christian life by means of the following meditation:

God not only gives gifts to me, but he literally gives himself to me. His is not only the Word in whom all things are created, but also the Word who becomes flesh and dwells with us. He gives himself to me so that his Body and Blood become the food and drink of my life. He pours out upon me his Spirit so that I can cry "Abba." God loves me so much that I literally become a dwelling place or a temple of God—growing in an ever-deepening realization of the image and likeness of God, which remains the glory of the creation of man and woman.

If I were to make only a reasonable response, what could I do? Moved by love, I may find that I can respond best in words like . . .

Take, Lord, and receive all my liberty, my memory, my understanding, and my entire will—all that I have and call my own. You have given it all to me. To you, Lord, I return it. Everything is yours; do with it what you will. Give me only your love and your grace. That is enough for me.[9]

A Scripture Reflection,

"This, then, is what I pray, kneeling before the Father, from whom every fatherhood, in heaven or on earth, takes its name. In the abundance of his glory may he, through his Spirit, enable you to grow firm in power with regard to your inner self, so that Christ may live in your hearts through faith, and then, planted in love and built on love, with all God's holy people you will have the strength to

---

[9] David L. Fleming, S.J., op. cit. p. 89.

grasp the breadth and the length, the height and the depth, so that, knowing the love of Christ, which is beyond knowledge, you may be filled with the utter fullness of God.

"Glory be to him whose power, working in us, can do infinitely more than we can ask or imagine; glory be to him from generation to generation in the Church and in Christ Jesus for ever and ever. Amen" (Eph 3:14-21).

7

Praying With and for Others

We often wonder what heaven and hell are like. The following image addresses that question in parable form:

> Heaven and hell are the same place. Everyone is standing around a banquet table. The table is overflowing with the most delectable food. People can't wait to enjoy the feast.
>
> Everyone in both heaven and hell is told that the food can be eaten only with a spoon. Each person is provided with an eight-foot spoon. The people in heaven are deliriously happy while the people in hell are totally frustrated and unhappy. Why? Well, those in hell are so used to going it alone that they unsuccessfully try to feed themselves—an impossible task with an eight-foot spoon! Those in heaven, on the other hand, eat to their hearts' content because they use their overly long spoons to feed one another.

True Christian prayer is a foretaste of heaven. It helps us discover that we don't stand alone before God. We are brothers and sisters who go to our Father together with our brother Jesus united in the Holy Spirit.

Christian prayer is communal. Jesus came so that we might be one. At the Last Supper he prayed:

> May they all be one,
> just as, Father, you are in me and I am in you,

so that they also may be in us,
so that the world may believe it was you who
    sent me (Jn 17:21).

Sometimes we pray alone, but Christian prayer is never just between one person and God. By virtue of our baptism, our prayers are united to those of the Lord Jesus and to those of the entire Christian family to which we belong.

INTERCESSORY PRAYER

Have you ever asked anyone to pray for you? Do others rely on you for prayers? Do you appreciate the value of prayer for others—or for yourself?

Some people don't value prayers of petition because they don't see the results of their prayer. Perhaps they prayed for a cancer-stricken relative, and the relative died. Or they prayed for good weather on their vacation, and it rained. Or they asked God to help them in their work situation, and they were fired.

Yet most of us have experienced the power of prayer for others. Perhaps we prayed for an alcoholic relative, and the person joined Alcoholics Anonymous. Or we prayed that a friend in a difficult situation would be helped, and the situation was resolved. Many times our prayers are answered—the way we want them to be.

My most heartfelt prayer was answered. I remember the day well. My wife had been in labor with our firstborn for 36 hours. Dilation was not taking place the way it should have so the doctor tried to deliver. He spent what seemed an eternity attempting to turn the baby who was in a breech position. Finally, he came to me in the delivery room and asked me what he should do. He was ashen white; his hands were shaking. Should he break my son's legs (his feet were in his mouth) in which case the baby might well die of shock? Or should he attempt an emergency caesarean section, but with no guarantee that my wife, who had already lost a great deal of blood, would survive?

Sensing the desperate situation, my mother-in-law fainted. My legs turned to jelly and my stomach did somersaults. I was paralyzed with fear. I don't remember exactly what I told the doctor, but it was something to the effect of his doing what he could to save both of them. One vivid memory, though, was my question, "But just please tell me, how much longer will you be?" He said perhaps half an hour.

I had been married a year almost to the day. In that year my wife and I had trained for the lay missions in Peru only to have the mission close the very month we finished our training. We tried to get placed with another mission in this country, but no one would have a lay couple ready to give birth to a child. I was terribly disappointed—with the missions and most especially with the Lord for seeming to bar us from work we wanted to do for him. I was resentful, confused and somewhat bitter.

But I turned to God on this day. And from the depths of my being I prayed—frightened, confused, hurting. Over and over I begged the Lord to spare my child and my wife.

A half hour went by. Then an hour. I was sure that something dreadful had happened. In desperation I continued to pour out my soul to the Lord.

After an hour and a half the doctor re-emerged from the operating room. With him came my new son and the jubilant news that both mother and baby were going to make it. And they did. There were complications, but both are healthy today, 16 years later.

The doctor was the head obstetrician at the hospital. He had delivered thousands of babies. About a week after the delivery he told me that it was a miracle that both my son and wife were alive. It was highly unlikely that either would have survived had the delivery taken place in Peru.

I also believe my prayers resulted in a miracle. The Lord did answer my prayers!

At times, though, our prayers don't seem to be answered. Why not? Doesn't the Lord teach us quite plainly in the Sermon on the Mount:

> "Ask, and it will be given to you; search, and you will find; knock, and the door will be opened to you. Everyone who asks receives; everyone who searches finds; everyone who knocks will have the door opened" (Mt 7:7-8).

It is not easy to say why our prayers are sometimes not answered the way we would like them to be. St. James offers one possible reason—a lack of faith in the one who prays:

> But the prayer must be made with faith, and no trace of doubt, because a person who has doubts is like the waves thrown up in the sea by the buffeting of the wind. That sort of person, in two minds, inconsistent in every activity, must not expect to receive anything from the Lord (Jas 1:6-8).

Many good Christians suffer from the infection of doubt. Its antidote is to pray like the anguished father who begged Jesus to cure his child: "I have faith. Help my lack of faith!" (Mk 9:24).

A second reason God's responses to our prayers don't always seem to go our way is simply because we don't understand everything about God's kingdom, about his plan for us. God does answer all of our prayers; it is just that we don't always recognize or want to recognize God's answer. No, after all, can be an answer too! For example, I didn't fully understand God's no to my fervent desire and prayer to be a lay missionary in Peru. But as subsequent events unfolded and in the context of prayer I discovered that the Lord really did answer my prayer. His no to my will became a yes to the life of my wife and son.

I tend to forget the petition in the Lord's Prayer where Jesus teaches us to pray "Thy will be done." If we mean that we want the Father's will to be done, then our prayers will be answered:

> Our fearlessness towards him consists in this,
> that if we ask anything in accordance with his will
> he hears us.
> And if we know that he listens to whatever we ask
>   him,
> we know that we already possess whatever we have
>   asked of him (1 Jn 5:14-15).

Trappist Basil Pennington, a modern guide in the ways to pray, writes:

> God will give us whatever we want, asking in prayer—
> what we truly want, not what we say we want or even
> think we want. God listens to the heart, not to the
> lips. He knows, too, how limited our understanding
> and knowledge. He sees our truest desires and knows
> how they can best be fulfilled. And this is what he
> grants. We may not see it at the moment, but we will
> in time. . . . If God seems to be saying "No" to some
> prayers, it is because he is saying "Yes" to the deepest
> prayer of our hearts.[1]

God is an all-loving Creator who cares deeply for his creation and especially for us, his children. But we must allow God the freedom to respond to our prayers in the way that is best for us and all others involved. We may never understand why our prayers are not answered the way we want them to be. But we can be sure of one thing: God loves us.

So, why should we pray for one another? Simply because that is what the Lord himself did and continues to do

---

[1] Basil Pennington, O.C.S.O., *Challenges in Prayer* (Wilmington, Delaware: Michael Glazier, Inc., 1982), pp. 61-62.

today. As St. Paul writes in Romans:

> Are we not sure that it is Christ Jesus, who died—yes
> and more, who was raised from the dead and is at
> God's right hand—and who is adding his plea for us?
> (Rom 8:34).

Jesus continues to be concerned about us today as he intercedes on our behalf before the Father. He invites us to show this same concern for others, to pray for their needs. He empowers us to join him in pleading our causes before his Father and our Father.

> In all your prayer and entreaty keep praying in the
> Spirit on every possible occasion. Never get tired of
> staying awake to pray for all God's holy people (Eph
> 6:18).

Clearly we are instructed to pray for our needs and the needs of others. Jesus himself said,

> "Whatever you ask for in my name I will do,
> so that the Father may be glorified in the Son.
> If you ask me for anything in my name,
> I will do it" (Jn 14:13-14).

Prayer for others—intercessory prayer—is prayer that can spill over into active concern for others. When we pray for others, we may be prompted to *do* something for them. Prayer is a process of learning to listen and respond to God. And Jesus told us that when we listen, pray for and respond to our neighbors—our brothers and sisters—we are responding to him:

> "In truth I tell you, in so far as you did this to one of
> the least of these brothers of mine, you did it to me"
> (Mt 25:40).

To pray for others is to be truly compassionate. When we allow the concerns, anxieties, struggles and worries of others to enter our awareness before the Lord, we forget ourselves. Our heart becomes one with theirs; we have compassion. Our Lord had compassion for us. He asks his friends to share in his compassion, to become one with others.

PRAYING WITH OTHERS

An excellent way to experience the power of praying for others is to pray *with* others. The value of this kind of prayer is stressed by Jesus himself:

> "In truth I tell you once again, if two of you on earth agree to ask anything at all, it will be granted to you by my Father in heaven. For where two or three meet in my name, I am there among them" (Mt 18:19-20).

When we join with others in prayer, we acknowledge that we are members of God's family. We support one another, not as isolated individuals, but as members of the Lord's body. We depend on one another for concern, love and encouragement. Many people find it easier to pray with others; when we make a commitment to pray with others on a regular basis, it sometimes helps us be more faithful to our prayer.

Prayer Groups

Religious communities, of course, provide time for communal prayer, but there are also many opportunities for lay people. Your parish may have a prayer group that meets on a regular basis or a Legion of Mary or sodalist group that prays the Rosary together. Lunch-time prayer groups are possible in business places. Or you might want to start a prayer group yourself. If so, discuss the following questions at the first meeting of your group. Other questions may well occur to you; discuss those too.

- How often should we meet and for how long?
- How large should the group be?
- Should we take turns leading the group?

- Should each session have a definite theme or should we just spend quiet time meditating together?

- Should we end our prayer time with a social period?

A popular format for prayer groups includes reading and reflecting on God's word. There are three stages to this kind of group prayer.

Stage 1: Reading God's Word

Choose a scripture passage. Notify the members of the group so they can read and reflect on the passage before the meeting.

When the group meets, you might wish to mention a certain intention for which the session will be offered; for example, for the health of a member's relative. You might also begin by singing a song or playing a recording if the group is comfortable with that. Choose music that relates to the theme of the scripture reading.

After the song, ask one person to read the chosen passage aloud, slowly and prayerfully. The others may want to close their eyes to help them concentrate as they listen to God's word.

Stage 2: Reflection on the Word of God

After a period of silence (or quiet background music), invite the participants to share their thoughts on the scripture passage. No one should feel obligated to share, however. And don't be afraid of silent intervals. Periods of silence are quite normal in group prayer sessions and add to the quality of the sharing. At this stage, the participants are directing their thoughts and impressions to one another, discussing the passage and sharing personal reactions. The participants should respect and try to learn from what others say.

Stage 3: Shared Prayer

The group can move into this third stage in a number of ways: by singing a song or hymn related to the passage, by enjoying a few minutes of silence, by rereading the passage, by playing quiet background music.

Shared prayer should take place spontaneously. Any participant who wishes to do so simply vocalizes his or her prayer. Simplicity is the key word for shared prayer. If the group is seated in a circle, each person can have the opportunity to offer a prayer in turn, but no one should feel compelled to do so. It is usually a good idea to signal the end of the shared prayer time with a short petition like, "We pray to the Lord," to which the participants respond, "Lord, hear our prayer" or some similar response.

Again, moments of silence between prayers can add to the richness of the prayer session.

Conclude with a song, a spontaneous concluding prayer or the recitation of the Our Father.

Prayer Partners

Finding a prayer partner to pray with us at a given time is another way to practice shared prayer. The most logical choice is a close friend, but someone else—a member of our family, a shut-in, a colleague—can be equally suitable. We can follow any format that seems comfortable to us: praying silently together, reading and reflecting on scripture, reciting the Rosary or other traditional prayer, reading and reflecting on passages from spiritual writings.

PRAYING THE EUCHARISTIC LITURGY

The greatest Christian prayer, of course, is the Mass. Through the eucharistic celebration we pray with and for others, just as Jesus at the Last Supper asked us to do.

When we gather at Mass, we are celebrating our identity as children of a loving Father and brothers and sisters of a generous Savior. We gather to pray—to deepen our friendship with the Lord—to praise God, to offer thanks, to ask for forgiveness and to ask God to meet our daily needs.

As we pray the Eucharist, we are reminded of a number of important truths. We recall that we are a community, a family who needs to gather together for strength and mutual encouragement to live Jesus' life. We are reminded that Jesus Christ has died, is risen and will come again. The Mass offers us the opportunity to share in the life of the risen Jesus as we receive him in communion. This invitation to receive the Lord and deepen our friendship with him strengthens us as a community. And this Christian family meal in Jesus' name both enables and challenges us to go out into the world to serve as Jesus served.

The eucharistic celebration, like all prayer, provides us with an opportunity to draw closer to God on our journey through life. The Eucharist is truly a celebration and, as a celebration, is very much a *public* affair. We don't pray the Eucharist by withdrawing from life, by escaping the world. Rather, as a community we engage ourselves in celebrating the greatest of all mysteries of love, the Paschal Mystery.

When we go to Mass we are entering into the Paschal Mystery of Jesus Christ, that is, we are celebrating, remembering and re-enacting the life, death and resurrection of the Lord. The sacred actions, the joyful singing, the proclamation of God's word, the offering of the gifts of our lives and our faith, and the reception of our lord in the midst of the community all powerfully remind us of his meaning and message.

The Eucharist is a most powerful sign of God's love; it challenges us to live in that love. The almighty God comes to us under the humble forms of bread and wine. We hear God's eternal word in the readings. We are reminded that the assembled Christian community is his body. As the community recalls and re-enacts the life, death and resurrection of Jesus celebrated in the sacred mysteries, the community is challenged to remember and live the Paschal Mystery in daily life.

Jesus' life of service and his message of peace culminated in the free gift of his life for all of us. The Lord surrendered his life in a supreme act of love and compassion for all people. Paradoxically, his death led to superabundant life. His resurrection shouts the good news of salvation—that sin and its greatest effect, death, have been conquered. The surrender of self for others—self-sacrificing love which may well lead to death—is the essence of the meaning of life. Love leads to true life, superabundant life. To love is to imitate the Lord. To love is to be an image of God.

The Eucharist is a celebration of love, a remembrance of love and a challenge of love—all in the context of communal prayer. The liturgy of the Mass both creates and celebrates Christian community, a primary fruit of responding to the Lord's love. But Christian community does not automatically happen. Our prayer for unity should flow out of affection for our fellow worshippers, a love for one another that is real because we have worked at getting to know one another. By becoming involved in the parish community we grow closer to those with whom we worship.

Praying the Eucharist

We can become so familiar with the form of the Mass that we fail to internalize its action. It is good occasionally to meditate on the institution of the Eucharist, to bring back into focus this essential Christian prayer:

1. Find a quiet place. Relax. Become aware of the presence of God.

2. Prayerfully read and meditate on Luke 22:14-20.

Place yourself in the scene. Vividly imagine what took place.

3. Write a journal reflection based on your meditation. You might address the reflection directly to Jesus.

In addition, many pray-ers meditate on the readings for the next day's Mass the evening before.

The Mass is an eloquent reminder that prayer is not something that is just between God and an individual. We come together to worship, to celebrate our brotherhood and sisterhood, and to receive the source of life, our Lord Jesus Christ. The Lord reminds us that we must take him out into the world. We must be broken for others just as he was broken for us. Prayer that does not translate into service of others is not true prayer. Jesus himself said:

> "It is not anyone who says to me, 'Lord, Lord,' who will enter the kingdom of Heaven, but the person who does the will of my Father in heaven" (Mt 7:21).

The Mass reminds us that because we have received the body of Christ we must *become* the body of Christ. We are his hands that touch and care for the sick, old and infirm; his feet that go out of their way to meet the lonely and befriend them; his understanding and forgiving glances that search for the hurting and hopeless in our midst.

To pray for and with others means that we must serve them, too. The closer we get to the Lord in prayer, the more we must be willing to imitate him, to "wash feet" as he did at the Last Supper. A popular image says it well. God is the hub of a wheel; we are the spokes. As we draw closer to the center, to God, we also come closer to each other. Proximity to the Lord God requires us to imitate his own life of service; there is no alternative.

Service doesn't "just happen." All too often we pass by opportunities for serving others; our intentions are good, but we let specific moments slip by. A frequent ex-

amination of conscience can help us heighten our awareness of our interactions with those we meet in our daily
lives.

1. What am I doing right now to serve others at
   home?

2. What am I doing right now to serve others at work?

3. Which area in my daily life currently provides an
   opportunity for service? How shall I respond to this
   opportunity? (Be specific.)

A Prayer Reflection

Reflect on the following words of novelist Albert Ca-
mus. Relate them to any service projects in which you are
currently involved.

> Don't walk in front of me,
> I may not follow.
> Don't walk behind me,
> I may not lead.
> Walk beside me,
> And just be my friend.

A Scripture Reflection

"You know that among the gentiles those they call their
rulers lord it over them, and their great men make their authority felt. Among you this is not to happen. No; anyone
who wants to become great among you must be your servant, and anyone who wants to be first among you must be
slave to all. For the Son of man himself came not to be
served but to serve, and to give his life as a ransom for
many" (Mk 10:42-45).

8
Some More Prayer Practices

The time we spend with the Lord in prayer is the most valuable part of our day. God demands very little of us—just that we slow down a bit so that we can become aware of the divine love we are offered. God does not shout at us. The divine presence in our lives is like a gentle breeze or a fresh, slowly flowing brook of crystal-clear water. God is there to give us life, to assure us that we are loved, to strengthen us for the journey. We need only stop to pay attention, to listen for the voice of God. We have discussed many forms of prayer in other chapters. In this chapter let us turn to some of the other traditional prayer practices which are often helpful on our journey with the Lord.

Ejaculations

Prayers don't have to be long. The Jesus Prayer is a powerful and brief prayer. One-line prayers sometimes say what we are thinking better than a host of words, and they can be used on many occasions. For example, when we offer an ejaculation before we begin a task, the task itself can become a prayer. A favorite ejaculation can also help us deal with distractions during our meditation or contemplation.

Here are some familiar ejaculations:

Jesus, my Lord and Savior, I love you.

Jesus, have mercy on me.

Lord, keep me from temptation.

My Jesus, mercy.

All glory, praise, honor and thanksgiving be to you,
O Lord Jesus.

Praise God!

Holy Spirit, enlighten me.

Mary, mother of God, pray for me.

There are many other phrases that are suitable ejaculations,
of course, or we can select a phrase of our own.

Stations of the Cross

We have already discussed the value of the imagination in helping us pray. The Stations of the Cross fully engage our imaginations as they focus our attention on the
passion, death and resurrection of Jesus.

The Stations of the Cross bring to mind the great gift
of God's love for us. Reflecting on Christ's passion helps us
appreciate how valuable we are in God's eyes. It also reaf-
firms the great mystery of our faith—through the death
and resurrection of our Lord Jesus Christ comes eternal life
for all of us.

This devotion grew out of the custom of Holy Land
pilgrims who used to walk the steps Jesus took from his
place of condemnation to Calvary. In most Catholic
churches, the stations are depicted around the church.
These stations are visual images to help us imagine the sufferings of Jesus. Usually there are 14 stations pictured. The
15th station, the resurrection, has been added in recent
years to underscore the Paschal Mystery, the fact that the

sufferings and death of Jesus led to his glorious resurrection. When we pray the Stations of the Cross—and there are several good booklets available to help us do so—we are reminded that the Lord also instructs us to enter into his passion, to pick up our own crosses daily. Praying the Stations of the Cross is an excellent way to reflect on what it means to follow Jesus.

The stations consist of a meditation on each of the following scenes:

1. Jesus Is Condemned to Death
2. Jesus Takes Up His Cross
3. Jesus Falls the First Time
4. Jesus Meets His Mother
5. Simon of Cyrene Helps Jesus Carry His Cross
6. Veronica Wipes the Face of Jesus
7. Jesus Falls the Second Time
8. Jesus Consoles the Women of Jerusalem
9. Jesus Falls the Third Time
10. Jesus Is Stripped of His Garments
11. Jesus Is Nailed to the Cross
12. Jesus Dies on the Cross
13. Jesus Is Taken Down From the Cross
14. Jesus Is Laid in the Tomb
15. The Resurrection of the Lord

Novena

The novena is another traditional devotion. A novena consists of the recitation of certain prayers over a period of nine days. The symbolism of the nine days refers to the period of time Mary and the apostles spent in prayer between the Lord's ascension and Pentecost.

Many times the novena is dedicated to Mary or to a saint with the faith and hope that he or she will intercede for the one making the novena. Novenas to St. Jude, St. Anthony, Our Lady of Perpetual Help and Our Lady of Lourdes remain popular.

Unfortunately, in some circles today novenas have a bad name. Some people have a mistaken notion about novenas. For example, you might have received a letter, usually unsigned, which told you that if you recited a particular novena, perhaps one to St. Jude, your requests were sure to be granted. You may have been urged to make copies of the letter and send them to your friends.

This approach to prayer is basically superstitious and unchristian. It reflects a belief that God can be manipulated, that he can be maneuvered into doing our will. Jesus himself warned against this when he said:

> "In your prayers do not babble as the gentiles do, for they think by using many words they will make themselves heard. Do not be like them; your Father knows what you need before you ask him" (Mt 6:7-8).

Prayer demands patience. The original novena of Mary and the apostles strongly reminds us of this truth. They waited patiently for nine days in the upper room for the gift of the Holy Spirit. Why did they have to wait? Perhaps because the Lord wished to teach them, and us, a most valuable lesson: It takes time for growth to take place. When we wait upon the Lord in a prayerful way, there is time for us to grow aware of God's action and presence in our lives.

> In waiting we become aware that all life, all goodness, all freedom, all joy, all love are gifts from God. In prayer we stand waiting to receive the abundant gifts of God, doing what we can to be receptive to these gifts.[1]

Litanies

Jesus taught us to pray fervently, continually and with perseverance. Litanies are a popular way to pray because

---

[1] Keith J. Egan, O. Carm., *What Is Prayer?* (Denville, New Jersey: Dimension Books, 1973), p. 25.

they help us to persist in prayer. Litanies are prayer in the form of responsive petitions; for example, this is a short excerpt from the Litany of Loreto:

Holy Mary,	pray for us.
Holy Mother of God,	pray for us.
Holy Virgin of virgins,	pray for us.
Mother of Christ,	pray for us.

Under a variety of titles, litanies typically invoke God, Jesus, Mary, St. Joseph and other saints. Examples of popular litanies are those of the Blessed Mother, the Holy Name, the Sacred Heart of Jesus, the Precious Blood, All Saints, St. Joseph and St. Anthony.

Pray the following litany, the "Divine Praises," slowly, reflecting on each phrase.

Blessed be God.
Blessed be his holy name.
Blessed be Jesus Christ, true God and true man.
Blessed be the name of Jesus.
Blessed be his most sacred heart.
Blessed be his most precious blood.
Blessed be Jesus in the most holy sacrament of
  the altar.
Blessed be the Holy Spirit, the Paraclete.
Blessed be the great mother of God,
  Mary most holy.
Blessed be her holy and immaculate conception.
Blessed be her glorious assumption.
Blessed be the name of Mary, virgin and mother.
Blessed be St. Joseph, her most chaste spouse.
Blessed be God in his angels and in his saints.

Fasting

In the Sermon on the Mount, Jesus teaches us about three sine qua nons of the Christian life—almsgiving, prayer and fasting. Significantly, these three Christian practices are linked together. Prayer is a search for union with God; almsgiving is a call to charity; fasting means self-denial. All three are essential for Christian life.

Almsgiving, which is symbolic of the loving service of others, demonstrates the authenticity and sincerity of our prayer. Fasting is a form of self-denial, of saying no to some good thing out of love for God; it can enrich our prayer life, our search for union with God. Fasting is a form of penance which helps us acquire the attitudes of Jesus.

In the traditional sense we typically think of fasting as staying away from all food for a certain period of time, for example, between meals. A contemporary understanding might broaden the definition of fasting to include other forms of self-discipline.

The liturgical season of Lent has traditionally been a good time for Christians to turn to acts of self-denial. For example, many people maintain the Lenten fast (eating only at the three meals of the day; meat only at the main meal; the other two meals to be light) although church law no longer requires this for all the days of Lent.

We can also abstain from certain foods, that is, stop eating them for a certain period of time. In their pastoral letter *The Challenge of Peace: God's Promise and Our Response,* the American bishops called upon American Catholics to eat less food and abstain from meat on Fridays as well as to engage in works of charity and service toward one another for the sake of peace. Acts of penance like fasting and abstaining are tangible signs that Christians are pilgrims, people who are on their way to the Father, in constant need of conversion.

Fasting and abstaining from certain foods that we especially enjoy can also demonstrate that we are not slaves to our appetites. In addition, when we fast or abstain, we hunger—at least for a time. This hunger can remind us of our absolute dependence on God. Everything we have and everything we are is a gift from God.

Fasting and abstaining can help discipline us. We develop our spiritual strength when we freely deny ourselves some good things. Self-denial can be a form of love for God and others. It can help us learn to be generous, to delay immediate gratification, and to develop empathy for the plight of the needy. To walk, however briefly, with "the least of these" reinforces our commitment to care for and about our brothers and sisters. Following Jesus and living the kind of life he calls us to live demand that we be prepared to sacrifice. Fasting and abstaining—joined with prayer—can aid us in our spiritual growth.

The Liturgy of the Hours

The Liturgy of the Hours is part of the official, public prayer of the church. Along with the celebration of the sacraments, the recitation of the Divine Office (*office* means "duty" or "obligation") helps render constant praise and thanksgiving to God.

The purpose of the Liturgy of the Hours is to make holy both the day and the night by praising God. It consists of five major divisions:

- An Hour of Readings
- Morning Praises
- Mid-day Prayers
- Vespers (Evening Prayers)
- Compline (a short Night Prayer)

Scriptural prayer, especially the psalms, is at the heart of the Liturgy of the Hours. Each day follows a separate pattern of prayer with themes closely tied in with the liturgical year and the feasts of the saints.

As the official prayer of the church, the Divine Office is faithfully recited on behalf of all of God's people by priests and others who have taken solemn vows. But more and more lay people have discovered the riches of this form of prayer and are deriving much spiritual benefit from it. A good way to begin is by praying the Morning Praises and the Vespers over a period of time.

Conclusion

In the Catholic tradition there are many other prayer practices: visiting the Blessed Sacrament; lighting votive candles as a symbolic reminder to the Lord of a petition; participating in a holy hour to commemorate the Lord's request in the Garden of Gethsemane for his apostles to remain awake with him for an hour; attending Forty Hours services; going to parish missions; making a retreat. All are helpful ways to grow in the spiritual life. Variety is sometimes the very spice we need when our prayer life seems stale.

As we come to the conclusion of this introduction to prayer, what final advice can I give? There are three points that I wish to make here:

• *Continue to read about prayer.*   There are many excellent books—both practical and understandable—that will help us on our journey. In the bibliography on pages 137-141 I have annotated a few of my favorite works. I think any of these would make excellent follow-up reading to this book.

• *Find a spiritual mentor.*   The spiritual director, to use the more traditional term, is a trustworthy Christian friend with whom we can share our prayer life. He or she can give us advice and encouragement for our spiritual journey. This mentor should be a devout person of prayer with whom we feel comfortable. Such a person is not always easy to find. You might ask a parish priest, a seasoned pray-er who has a director, a member of a religious order, or a staff member at a retreat house to recommend someone. Prayer can be a very private thing, but the Christian life is a communal life. We need the help, encouragement, support and advice of our Christian brothers and sisters. Anyone who prays on a regular basis knows the great value of sharing the journey to the Father with a prayer mentor.

• *Pray!*   Nothing can substitute for prayer itself. Experiment. There are many paths of prayer that Christians have taken on their spiritual journey. You are bound to find at least one of them to be a total delight, to be a way to enrich your life in the Lord.

My prayer for all readers of this book is that the Lord will show us the way to draw closer to him so that we might draw closer to our loved ones and be emboldened to serve others more faithfully. I also ask the Lord to grant us the privilege to meet each other in eternity. In the Holy Spirit, may he bless all of us on our common journey.

A Prayer Reflection

Light a small candle. Recall Jesus' words that he is the "light of the world." Become aware of the Lord's presence and reflect on the ways he brings light to your life. As the Holy Spirit for guidance in ways you can bring the light of Jesus to others.

A Scripture Reflection

"Always be joyful, then, in the Lord; I repeat, be joyful. Let your good sense be obvious to everybody. The Lord is near. Never worry about anything; but tell God all your desires of every kind in prayer and petition shot through with gratitude, and the peace of God which is beyond our understanding will guard your hearts and your thoughts in Christ Jesus. . . . Let your minds be filled with everything that is true, everything that is honorable, everything that is upright and pure, everything that we love and admire—with whatever is good and praiseworthy. Keep doing everything you learnt from me and were told by me and have heard or seen me doing. Then the God of peace will be with you'' (Phil 4:4-9).

Appendix

This appendix contains a brief review of some of the types of prayer discussed in the book and a compilation of some traditional prayers.

Four Kinds of Prayer

1. Adoration
2. Contrition
3. Thanksgiving
4. Supplication

Prayer as Recollection

1. Focus: Relax.
2. Insight: Ask the Holy Spirit for enlightenment.
3. Evaluate: Think about the past day.
4. Forgiveness: Ask the Lord for forgiveness.
5. Thanksgiving: Thank God for all that you have been given.

Jesus on Prayer

1. Keep it simple.
2. Pray with childlike faith.

3.   Be persistent.

4.   Pray with others.

5.   Pray with forgiveness in your heart.

6.   Pray with humility.

Making a Decision

1.   Speak to the Lord as to a friend. Ask for help.

2.   List each alternative, lining up the pros and cons.

3.   List values in each alternative.

4.   Consider the consequences of each alternative.

5.   Discuss your thoughts with your spiritual director, prayer partner or another Christian brother or sister.

6.   Ask again for the Lord's help and direction.

Meditation

1.   Relax: Find a peaceful place and posture.

2.   Observe: What is this? What is here?

3.   Reflect: What does this mean?

4.   Listen: What is this teaching me?

5.   Resolve: What can I do?

Or use St. Benedict's three-step method of sacred reading, meditation and prayer.

Contemplation

1.   Relax: Find a peaceful place and posture.

2.   Center: Perhaps use a word like *Jesus* to drive away distracting thoughts. The goal is to empty the mind of all thoughts.

3.   Rest: Sit calmly in the presence of the Lord.

Scriptural Prayer With Others

1. Read God's word.

2. Reflect on God's word.

3. Share prayer.

Traditional Prayers

Sign of the Cross

In the name of the Father,
and of the Son,
and of the Holy Spirit. Amen.

Our Father

Our Father,
who are in heaven,
hallowed be your name.
Your kingdom come,
Your will be done on earth as it is in heaven.
Give us this day our daily bread
and forgive us our trespasses
as we forgive those who trespass against us.
And lead us not into temptation,
but deliver us from evil.
For the kingdom, the power, and the glory are yours
now and forever. Amen.

Glory Be

Glory be to the Father,
and to the Son

and to the Holy Spirit,
as it was in the beginning,
is now,
and will be forever. Amen.

Hail Mary

Hail Mary, full of grace,
the Lord is with you.
Blessed are you among women
and blessed is the fruit of your womb, Jesus.
Holy Mary, mother of God,
pray for us sinners now
and at the hour of our death. Amen.

Memorare

Remember, O most gracious Virgin Mary,
that never was it known
that anyone who fled to your protection,
implored your help,
or sought your intercession was left unaided.
Inspired by this confidence,
I fly unto you,
O Virgin of virgins, my mother.
To you I come, before you I stand,
sinful and sorrowful.
O Mother of the Word incarnate,
despise not my petitions,
but in your mercy hear and answer me. Amen.

Hail, Holy Queen

Hail, holy Queen, mother of mercy,
our life, our sweetness and our hope.
To you do we cry,
poor banished children of Eve.
To you do we send up our sighs,

mourning and weeping in this valley of tears.
Turn then, O most gracious advocate,
your eyes of mercy toward us,
and after this exile
show us the blessed fruit of your womb, Jesus.
O clement, O loving, O sweet Virgin Mary.
Pray for us, O holy Mother of God,
that we may be made worthy of the promises of
Christ. Amen.

Morning Offering

O Jesus, through the Immaculate Heart of Mary, I offer
you my prayers, works, joys and sufferings of this day
in union with the holy sacrifice of the Mass throughout
the world. I offer them for all the intentions of your
sacred heart; the salvation of souls, reparation for sin,
the reunion of all Christians. I offer them for the intentions of our bishops and all members of the Apostle-
ship of Prayer and in particular for those recommended by our Holy Father this month. Amen.

Apostles' Creed

I believe in God, the Father almighty,
creator of heaven and earth.
I believe in Jesus Christ, his only Son, our Lord.
He was conceived by the power of the Holy
Spirit and born of the Virgin Mary.
He suffered under Pontius Pilate, was
crucified, died, and was buried.
He descended to the dead.
On the third day he rose again.
He ascended into heaven, and is seated at the
right hand of the Father.
He will come again to judge the living and the
dead.

I believe in the Holy Spirit,
>   the holy catholic Church,
>   the communion of saints,
>   the forgiveness of sins
>   the resurrection of the body,
>   and life everlasting. Amen.

Act of Faith

O my God, I firmly believe that you are one God in three divine Persons, Father, Son, and Holy Spirit; I believe that your divine Son became man and died for our sins, and that he will come to judge the living and the dead. I believe these and all the truths which the Holy Catholic Church teaches, because you have revealed them, who can neither deceive nor be deceived. Amen.

Act of Hope

O my God, relying on your infinite goodness and promises, I hope to obtain pardon of my sins, the help of your grace, and life everlasting, through the merits of Jesus Christ, my Lord and Redeemer. Amen.

Act of Love

O my God, I love you above all things, with my whole heart and soul, because you are all good and worthy of all my love. I love my neighbor as myself for the love of you. I forgive all who have injured me, and I ask pardon of all whom I have injured. Amen.

An Act of Contrition

My God, I am sorry for my sins with all my heart. In choosing to do wrong and failing to do good, I have sinned against you whom I should love above all things. I firmly intend, with your help, to do penance, to sin no more, and to avoid whatever leads me to sin. Our Savior Jesus Christ suffered and died for us. In his name, my God, have mercy. Amen.

The Angelus

The angel of the Lord declared unto Mary.
R: And she conceived by the Holy Spirit.
> Hail Mary . . .

Behold the handmaid of the Lord.
R: May it be done unto me according to your word.
> Hail Mary . . .

And the word was made flesh.
R: And dwelled among us.
> Hail Mary . . .

Pray for us, O holy mother of God.
R: That we may be made worthy of the promises of Christ.

Let us pray: We beseech you, O Lord, to pour out your grace into our hearts. By the message of an angel we have learned of the incarnation of Christ, your Son; lead us, by his passion and cross, to the glory of the resurrection. Through the same Christ our Lord. Amen.

Grace at Meals

Before Meals

Bless us, O Lord,
and these your gifts,
which we are about to receive from your bounty,
through Christ our Lord. Amen.

After Meals

We give you thanks, almighty God,
for these and all the gifts
which we have received

from your goodness,
through Christ our Lord. Amen.

Prayer for the Faithful Departed

Eternal rest grant unto them, O Lord.
R: And let perpetual light shine upon them.
May their souls and the souls of all the faithful departed, through the mercy of God, rest in peace.
R: Amen.

Canticle of Brother Sun

Most high, all-powerful, all good, Lord!
    All praise is yours, all glory, all honor
    And all blessing.
To you, alone, Most High, do they belong.
    No mortal lips are worthy
    To pronounce your name.
All praise be yours, my Lord, through all that you have made,
    And first my lord Brother Sun,
    Who brings the day; and light you give to us through him.
How beautiful is he, how radiant in all his splendor!
    Of you, Most High, he bears the likeness.
All praise be yours, my Lord, through Sister Moon and Stars;
    In the heavens you have made them, bright
    And precious and fair.
All praise be yours, my Lord, through Brothers Wind and Air,
    And fair and stormy, all the weather's moods,
    By which you cherish all that you have made.
All praise be yours, my Lord, through Sister Water,
    So useful, lowly, precious and pure.
All praise be yours, my Lord, through Brother Fire,
    Through whom you brighten up the night.

How beautiful is he, how gay! Full of power and
strength.
All praise be yours, my Lord, through Sister Earth, our
mother,
Who feeds us in her sovereignty and produces
Various fruits with colored flowers and herbs.
All praise be yours, my Lord, through those who grant
pardon
For love of you; through those who endure
Sickness and trial.
Happy those who endure in peace,
By you, Most High, they will be crowned.
All praise be yours, my Lord, through Sister Death,
From whose embrace no mortal can escape.
Woe to those who die in mortal sin!
Happy those She finds doing your will!
The second death can do no harm to them.
Praise and bless my Lord, and give him thanks,
And serve him with great humility.

Bibliography

What should you read next? I encourage you to read one of the spiritual classics discussed in Chapters 5 and 6 of this book or one of the two listed below. I also include below some modern works on prayer that I can highly recommend to you. They are excellent introductions to prayer that are clearly written and easy to understand. In addition, they contain many insights that are also helpful for the seasoned pray-er.

Classics

Juliana of Norwich. *Revelations of Divine Love*. Translated with an Introduction by M. L. Del Mastro. Garden City, New York: Doubleday, Image Books, 1977.

Today, Juliana of Norwich is a very popular English mystic noted for her joyousness and deep conviction that ours is a merciful God. A famous example of her spiritual perception can be seen in her contemplation of a little thing, the size of a hazel nut. In trying to understand it, it was revealed to her that "It is all that is made." You may wish to sample this insightful mystic.

St. Teresa of Avila. *The Collected Works of St. Teresa of Avila*, vol. 2. Translated by Kieran Kavanaugh, O.C.D. and Otilio Rodriguez, O.C.D. Washington, D.C.: Institute of Carmelite Studies, 1980.

As mentioned in Chapter 6, Teresa can be difficult. However, I think a beginner in prayer can read with great profit *The Way of Perfection*. Written for her nuns, it uses the Lord's Prayer as a path to meditation and contemplation.

Modern Works

Bloom, Anthony. *Beginning to Pray*. New York: Paulist Press, 1970.

A modern spiritual classic. Deep insights for the beginning pray-er.

Boulding, Maria. *Prayer: Our Journey Home*. Ann Arbor, Michigan: Servant Publications, 1980.

Thoughts about prayer with excellent reflections on intercessory prayer, on praying the psalms, on "ordinary" contemplative prayer, and on wholeness and healing.

Carretto, Carlo. *In Search of the Beyond*. Translated by Sarah Fawcett. Maryknoll, New York: Orbis Books, 1976.

A fascinating look at contemporary prayer by a modern spiritual master. Carretto is a disciple of the 20th-century mystic Charles de Foucauld. This book shows the connection between prayer and action, especially by applying the Beatitudes to Christian living.

Davidson, Graeme J. with Mary MacDonald. *Anyone Can Pray: A Guide to Methods of Christian Prayer*. New York: Paulist Press, 1983.

An excellent handbook on different ways to pray. Short, easy-to-read chapters treat topics like spontaneous prayer, traditional prayer forms, charismatic and Asian prayer techniques, and prayer with others.

de Mello, S.J., Anthony. *One Minute Wisdom*. Garden City, New York: Doubleday, 1986.

> Father de Mello teaches us how to pray using the mystical traditions of both the East and the West. His books—including *Sadhana: A Way to God, Song of the Bird* and *Wellsprings*—provide excellent material for meditation.

Doherty, Catherine de Hueck. *Poustinia*. Notre Dame, Indiana: Ave Maria Press, 1975.

> In writing about the *poustinia*, the prayer room of our heart, Catherine Doherty writes not so much about a prayer technique as about a journey into God. A good introduction to the Christian spirituality of the East.
> You may also want to read Doherty's *Soul of My Soul* (Ave Maria Press, 1985), the heart of her experience and reflections about prayer.

Evely, Louis. *We Dare to Say Our Father*. Translated by James Langdale. Garden City, New York: Doubleday, Image Books, 1975.

> Evely is one of the most popular spiritual writers of the past 30 years or so. This work contains some profound insights on the Lord's Prayer.

Farrell, S.T.L., Edward. *Prayer Is a Hunger*. Denville, New Jersey: Dimension Books, 1972.

> Farrell is a balanced teacher of prayer.

Finley, James. *The Awakening Call*. Notre Dame, Indiana: Ave Maria Press, 1984.

> An introduction to contemplative prayer through references to the spiritual classics, especially *The Cloud of Unknowing* and John of the Cross.

Green, S.J., Thomas. *Opening to God: A Guide to Prayer.* Notre Dame, Indiana: Ave Maria Press, 1977.

Father Green is one of the best authors writing about prayer today. After reading this introduction to prayer, try *When the Well Runs Dry: Prayer Beyond the Beginnings* (Ave Maria Press, 1979) or one of his other excellent books. As mentioned in Chapter 6, his *A Vacation With the Lord* is an invaluable aid in making an Ignatian retreat.

Groeschel, O.F.M. Cap., Benedict J. *Listening at Prayer*. New York: Paulist Press, 1983.

An excellent, simple guide to listening, a major key to encountering God in a fresh way.

Link, Mark. *You: Prayer for Beginners and Those Who Have Forgotten How*. Niles, Illinois: Argus Communications, 1976.

A delightful seven-week course on prayer that covers the many different types of prayer. A most helpful introduction by a popular Jesuit teacher.

Main, John. *Moment of Christ: The Path of Meditation*. New York: Crossroad, 1984.

A simple, practical guide to meditation.

Maloney, S.J., George A. *Journey Into Contemplation*. Locust Valley, New York: Living Flame Press, 1983.

This is an excellent guide for the beginner who wants to learn contemplative prayer. Those interested in contemplative prayer, especially the Jesus Prayer, will want to read his *Prayer of the Heart* (Notre Dame, Indiana: Ave Maria Press, 1981).

Muto, Susan Annette. *Meditation in Motion*. New York: Doubleday, 1986.

Is spirituality the luxury of the religious elite, or are all of us called to a life of prayer? Susan Muto offers insights into this question and related topics as well as providing meditations and prayers to inspire the reader.

Nouwen, Henri J. M. *The Genesee Diary: Report From a Trappist Monastery*. Garden City, New York: Doubleday, Image Books, 1976.

There is something intimate and engrossing about reading another person's prayer journal. We learn from the halts and shortcomings of others as well as from their triumphs and joys. Father Nouwen is an extremely popular spiritual guide. We can gain many insights into the prayer life from his works. Beginners might find *With Open Hands* (Notre Dame, Indiana: Ave Maria Press, 1977) especially valuable. Those interested in praying with icons will find inspiration in *Behold the Beauty of the Lord* (Notre Dame, Indiana: Ave Maria Press, 1987).

Pennington, O.C.S.O., Basil. *Challenges in Prayer*. Wilmington, Delaware: Michael Glazier, Inc., 1982.

A solid introduction to prayer with easy-to-understand insights on contemplation. I also recommend Father Pennington's *Centering Prayer* (Garden City, New York: Doubleday, Image Books, 1980).